continued on back

Survival Probabilities

Survival Probabilities

The goal of risk theory

HILARY L. SEAL

Ecole Polytechnique Fédérale de Lausanne

JOHN WILEY & SONS
Chichester · New York · Brisbane · Toronto

Library of Congress Cataloging in Publication Data:
Seal, Hilary L
    Survival probabilities, the goal of risk theory
    (Wiley series in probability and mathematical
statistics)
    1.   Risk (Insurance).   I.   Title.
HG8053.S4   368   78–8599

ISBN 0 471 99683 1

Typeset in Great Britain by Preface Ltd., Salisbury, Wilts
and printed by Unwin Brothers Ltd., The Gresham
Press, Old Woking, Surrey.

To Hiskie, who helped

Preface

I was introduced to what is today called Risk Theory, and in those days had an adjectival prefix 'collective', by the latter part of Harald Cramér's beautiful 78-page article in English in the 1930 *festskrift* of the Swedish insurance company Skandia. Like others before me I did not find Filip Lundberg's stochastic model of a risk business, carefully interpreted and developed though it was by Cramér, at all easy to understand and was immensely relieved to read Ingvar Laurin's 'popularization' in the 1930 Scandinavian actuarial journal. In the late thirties I was drawn away from the insurance business and it was not until 1967 that Frank Anscombe, Chairman of the Statistics Department at Yale University, suggested to me that I should give a course to graduate students on the stochastic problems of a risk business.

My book (Seal, 1969) was the result and a then current assessment of Risk Theory is to be found in its Chapter 4. Imagine my surprise when I came to write it and restudy what until after the war had been a strictly Swedish subject, that I discovered I couldn't find a single numerical probablity of insurance company ruin (namely, negative free capital and surplus) other than in an infinite time span. And even Swedish insurance companies cannot plan to last forever! The principal reason for this dearth of numerical results was the difficulty of developing reasonable approximate formulas and the great complexity of 'exact' results.

This has all been changed by the general availability of fast electronic computers and the simplicity of devising programs for them. Since I wrote my Chapter 4 I have spent much of my time trying to produce numerical probabilities of ruin for what I believe are realistic models of nonlife insurance companies. This book describes the results and their associated computer programs. The probability of an insurance company surviving a limited time period during which the annual number of claims is expected to be reasonably constant but which could become enormous can now be calculated quite easily and accurately. It is this probability I propose to discuss.

My sincere thanks go to Robert E. Beard, Gunnar Benktander and Gregory C. Taylor who kindly read my manuscript and made a number of helpful suggestions. My deep gratitude to N. Uma Prabhu is evident throughout Chapter 4.

Notes

(1) If reference is made to a relation in another chapter that chapter number precedes the relation number. For example, in any chapter other than the first, (1.10) refers to relation (10) in Chapter 1.

(2) All the computer runs mentioned in this monograph were made on the CDC 6500 of the Ecole Polytechnique Fédérale de Lausanne. Reduced computation times would, of course, be obtained on a larger, faster computer.

(3) I would like to thank Professor Hans Bühlmann, editor of the Swiss actuarial journal, for permission to reproduce Tables 2.4, 2.5 and 2.6 from Seal (1972*a*). My thanks also go to Dr. Henry Verbeek, editor of the *Astin Bulletin*, for permission to take Table 5.1 from Seal (1978).

Contents

CHAPTER I

Historical Introduction

THE RANDOM VARIABLES Y AND T

If one makes an abstraction of the operation of a nonlife insurance company one is left with a series of epochs $t_1, t_2, t_3, \ldots$ at which a claim occurred (and was immediately paid!), together with the concomitant monetary amounts of claim $y_1, y_2, y_3, \ldots$. As a first step in the production of a mathematical model of such a company it is reasonable to suggest that, apart from monetary inflation which poses a problem that we will ignore, the amounts of claim should not be related either to each other or to the epochs at which they occur. It is quickly seen that a histogram of the frequencies with which claims of given size occur should then indicate a regular curve for the distribution of claims from the smallest to the largest claim size. In other words, the claim sizes should have a probability distribution such that the probability of observing a claim size Y less than or equal to y is a continuous function $B(y)$, called the distribution function (df) of Y, that increases steadily and continuously with y. We assume that $B(0) = 0$ and $B(\infty) = 1$.

Although the conceptual details are, perhaps, a little more opaque it may be suggested that the *intervals* of time between claims, namely $t_2 - t_1, t_3 - t_2, \ldots$, should also have a probability distribution and that the probability of such an interval T being less than or equal to t should be continuous in t. We will write it $A(t)$ with $A(0) = 0$ and $A(\infty) = 1$. Note that the interval between 'now' (time zero) and the first claim, namely t_1, is *not* a proper member of the interval series so that, in a notation that hardly needs definition,

$$\text{Prob}\{t_1 \leqslant t\} \neq A(t) \tag{1}$$

– although the mere writing of this inequality makes us wonder whether there may not be some 'peculiar' $A(t)$ for which the inequality becomes an equality. (There is.)

We observe that we cannot categorically state that the successive time intervals are independent. Although $A(\cdot)$ is invariate for every interval there may be some sort of dependence between a set of interval lengths.

The asymmetry of the distribution of intervals between claims, requiring us always to be on the lookout for the probability on the left-hand side of (1), has

1

resulted in attention being paid to another function of claim occurrence epochs. Suppose we were to ask for the probability that $N(t)$ claims, with $N(t) =$ $0, 1, 2, \ldots$, occur in an interval of time extending from now to epoch t, which we write $(0,t)$. This probability automatically allows for the intuitively shorter interval to the first claim as well as for the following intervals which we will assume to be equal *on the average*. We will write

$$\text{Prob}\{N(t) = n\} \equiv \text{Pr}\{N(t) = n\} = p_n(t)$$

noting that a minuscule has been adopted for the probability of a single event (n claims) as compared with our previous majuscules for the probabilities of whole sets of events.

BARROIS AND DORMOY

The foregoing discussion provides a complete stochastic (probabilistic) model of the operation of a nonlife insurance business. Already in Barrois (1835) we find the concept of the probability that a building is struck by a fire distinguished from the amount consumed by the fire once it has occurred. In the Bohlmann–du Motel (1909) encyclopedia article on life assurance the probability density function of the size S of a claim in 'assurance des objets' is written as $\phi(S)$ where S can vary from zero to a maximum M, the sum insured. It is commented that cases where the data are sufficient to determine the form of $\phi(\cdot)$ are rare but that the Normal law is unlikely to apply. In life assurance S is fixed at the sum insured M and the probabilities of a claim are the rates of mortality which vary with the age attained of the life insured.

When claims and the time intervals between them occur independently and at random the probability that an interval greater than t arises between two claim epochs is analogous to the probability that a new born child lives to at least age t according to Dormoy's (1878) survival formula, namely $e^{-\lambda t}$ where λ is the intensity of mortality (or, in our case, the intensity of claims) at any age (epoch), and where time is reckoned in units of one year. Since the probability of death (a claim) at or before t is the complement of the survival probability we have

$$A(t) = 1 - e^{-\lambda t}$$

and will now prove that in this case we may measure t from an arbitrary time origin *or* from a claim occurrence.

Starting at a given claim epoch the probability that the interval to the first claim thereafter exceeds t_1 is

$$\text{Pr}\{T > t_1\} = e^{-\lambda t_1}$$

where, as already supposed, T is the random variable representing an interval length.

Similarly, the probability that the interval between two claims exceeds $t_0 + t_1$ is

$$\text{Pr}\{T > t_0 + t_1\} = e^{-\lambda(t_0 + t_1)}$$

Finally, knowing that at an arbitrary time origin the interval to the next claim has already equalled t_0 (or, in other words, the claim prior to the time origin occurred at time $-t_0$) we have

$$\Pr\{T > t_0 + t_1 \mid T > t_0\} \equiv \frac{\Pr\{T > t_0 + t_1\}}{\Pr\{T > t_0\}} = \frac{e^{-\lambda(t_0 + t_1)}}{e^{-\lambda t_0}}$$

$$= e^{-\lambda t_1} = \Pr\{T > t_1\}$$

The probability distribution of incomplete intervals to the next claim, measuring from an arbitrary time origin, is thus the same as the probability distribution of complete intervals between claims. It is easily shown that $e^{-\lambda t}$ is the only form for $1 - A(t)$ for which the foregoing derivation holds.

FILIP LUNDBERG

The above abstract model of a nonlife insurance company in which individuals are covered for insurance for an interval for which they have paid a premium, seems rather obvious by today's standards. But the fusing of ideas expressed by Barrois and those of the actuaries who were contemporaries of, and even antedated, Dormoy was not achieved until Lundberg (1903). This was a doctoral thesis at Uppsala University and was explicitly based on the foregoing ideas with the special (Dormoy) form for $A(\cdot)$ and the general form for $B(\cdot)$. At the commencement of the thesis Lundberg sets out to derive an equation for $f(\cdot, t)$, the frequency (or density) function of $X(t)$, the aggregate claims through epoch t. He obtained

$$f(x, t + dt) = \lambda dt \int_0^x f(x - y, t) \, dB(y) + (1 - \lambda dt) f(x, t) \tag{2}$$

where the first term on the right hand side represents the probability of a claim at epoch t, namely λdt, the size of which is y (independently of t); the second term accounts for the case where there is no claim at epoch t. In (2) we have slightly edited Lundberg who chose λ^{-1} as the unit of time so that λdt became dt, and who suppressed t in the density function $f(x, t)$. [In Cramér (1969) f is mistakenly written as a distribution function.] We have also inserted limits in the integral that conform to nonlife insurance. To the writer the concept of $B(\cdot)$ is much less natural when applied to the sums at risk in a life insurance or annuity portfolio. And he is dubious about the exponential form for $A(\cdot)$ when lives are insured. Lundberg does not say he is limiting himself to life insurance but he wrote the thesis while employed by the Förenade life insurance company and the actuaries of those days were almost exclusively practising in life insurance where level premiums were paid for long terms to cover risks that gradually increased. Laurin's (1930) article, for example, has exclusively life insurance examples.

With the minor differences remarked upon Lundberg rewrote (2) as

$$\frac{1}{\lambda} \cdot \frac{f(x, t + dt) - f(x, t)}{dt} = \frac{1}{\lambda} \cdot \frac{\partial f(x, t)}{\partial t}$$

$$= \int_0^x f(x - y, t)dB(y) - f(x, t) \tag{3}$$

an integro-differential equation for $f(x, t)$ where $B(\cdot)$ is known.

THE POISSON PROCESS

He only solved this equation for the special case where every claim has the same size, unity. In this case

$$B(y) = \begin{cases} 0 & y < 1 \\ 1 & y \geqslant 1 \end{cases}$$

and, writing p for f and n in lieu of x, (3) becomes

$$\frac{1}{\lambda} \cdot \frac{\partial p(n, t)}{\partial t} = p(n - 1, t) - p(n, t) \quad n = 1, 2, 3, \ldots \tag{4}$$

Consider the identity

$$\frac{\partial e^{\lambda t} p(n, t)}{\partial t} = e^{\lambda t} \frac{\partial p(n, t)}{\partial t} + \lambda e^{\lambda t} p(n, t)$$

and use (4) on the right hand side to get

$$\frac{\partial e^{\lambda t} p(n, t)}{\partial t} = \lambda e^{\lambda t} p(n - 1, t)$$

so that, on integrating from zero to t,

$$p(n, t) = \lambda e^{-\lambda t} \int_0^t e^{\lambda u} p(n - 1, u) du \tag{5}$$

since we may assume that $p(n, 0) = 0$ — no claims accrued at the time origin.
If we revert to (2) for $n = 0$ in our special case we get

$$p(0, t + dt) = (1 - \lambda dt) p(0, t)$$

or

$$\frac{\partial p(0, t)}{\partial t} = -\lambda p(0, t)$$

and

$$p(0, t) = e^{-\lambda t} \tag{6}$$

Putting $n = 1$ in (5)

$$p(1, t) = \lambda e^{-\lambda t} \int_0^t e^{\lambda u - \lambda u} \, du = \lambda t e^{-\lambda t}$$

then $n = 2$ in (5) gives

$$p(2, t) = \lambda e^{-\lambda t} \int_0^t e^{\lambda u} (\lambda u e^{-\lambda u}) du = \frac{(\lambda t)^2}{2} e^{-\lambda t}$$

and, inductively,

$$p(n, t) = e^{-\lambda t} \frac{(\lambda t)^n}{n!} \quad n = 0, 1, 2, 3 \ldots \tag{7}$$

This is Lundberg's result and the derivation, from (2) through (7), is that frequently used to obtain the Poisson law from a homogeneous (constant) intensity of occurrence, λ, in a stochastic process (e.g. Khintchine, 1933; Bhat, 1972). We note that $p(n, t)$ is what we called

$$p_n(t) = \Pr\{N(t) = n\}$$

earlier in this chapter. In this Poisson case

$$E\{N(t)\} = \lambda t.$$

LUNDBERG'S FORMULA FOR $F(x, t)$, THE df OF AGGREGATE CLAIMS

Cramér (1969) points out that Lundberg regarded $B(\cdot)$ in (2) as a function of t even though this was not shown by his notation. When $B(\cdot)$ could be regarded as time invariant — and nearly all work since that of Lundberg has used this assumption — Lundberg (1919) stated that (2) was satisfied by

$$f(x, t) = \sum_{n=1}^{\infty} p_n(t) b^{n*}(x) \tag{8}$$

where

$$b(y) = \frac{dB(y)}{dy} = b^{1*}(y)$$

and

$$b^{n*}(y) = \int_0^y b^{(n-1)*}(y - z) \, b(z) dz \quad n = 2, 3, 4, \ldots \tag{9}$$

Cramér (1969) says that Lundberg preferred to use (2) in his work but subsequent writers have invariably utilized (8) either as it stands or in the form of a distribution function, namely

$$F(x, t) = \int_0^x f(y, t)dy + f(0, t)$$

$$= \sum_{n=0}^{\infty} p_n(t)B^{n^*}(x) \tag{10}$$

with

$$B^{0^*}(y) = \begin{cases} 0 & y < 0 \\ 1 & y \geqslant 0 \end{cases}$$

$$B^{1^*}(y) = B(y)$$

and

$$B^{n^*}(y) = \int_0^y B^{(n-1)^*}(y - z)\, dB(z) \quad n = 2, 3, 4, \ldots \tag{11}$$

Since $B^{n^*}(\cdot)$ is the distribution function of the aggregate of n claim amounts (see, for example, Kendall and Stuart, 1977, Section 11.8) (10) has a simple interpretation. The probability of an aggregate claim size less than or equal to x in the interval $(0, t)$ depends on how many claims have occurred to contribute to this aggregate. If n claims have occurred, probability $p_n(t)$, the probability of their causing a claim aggregate not in excess of x is $B^{n^*}(x)$. Relation (10) follows. It is scarcely necessary to point out that the iterative procedure required in (9) or (11) would tax the resources of even a very fast computer and that, in general, some other procedure will have to be found for the numerical evaluation of (8) or (10).

THE SPIELFONDS AND RUIN OF THE COMPANY

In Lundberg (1909) we see the development of an important new idea (Cramér, 1969). The aggregate net premium payable during the interval $(0, t)$ to the nonlife insurance company we have imagined is

$$E\{X(t)\} = E\{N(t)\}E(Y)$$

where Y is the random variable representing the size of an individual claim. If we agree to measure money in units of the average claim size then $E(Y) = 1$. Hence the net premium payable to the company in $(0, t)$ is

$$E\{X(t)\} = E\{N(t)\} = \lambda t$$

in our Poisson case. It is widely recognized that a gambling casino must pay the punters less than their 'fair' prize if it is not to be ruined in the long run. Similarly here we 'load' the net premium with a risk loading that is conveniently assumed to be 100η % of the net premium itself. The risk loaded premium in our case is thus

$$(1 + \eta)\lambda t$$

Lundberg, who now explicitly mentions that nonlife as well as life insurance is concerned, proposed that the insurance company should set up a risk reserve (Spielfonds) into which it would pay risk-loaded premiums as they were received and from which it would pay claims. Writing this reserve as $R(t)$ at epoch t

$$R(t) = R(0) + (1 + \eta)\lambda t - X(t) \tag{12}$$

where $R(0) = w$ is the initial risk reserve, namely the initial free capital. Lundberg was interested in the probability that the *Spielfonds* would always remain positive, namely in what he called (in German) the *Soliditätszahl*. Today this probability is called the probability of nonruin in an unlimited period, the qualifying clause sometimes being omitted. Of course, with a non-zero risk loading η the expected value of $R(\cdot)$ grows without bound and Lundberg devoted substantial effort to deal with this problem, e.g. by letting η decrease as $R(\cdot)$ increases (Cramér, 1969). If survival of the company is only to be considered for finite, even small, values of t, we may well write $\eta = 0$ and absorb what would otherwise be the maximum receivable risk loadings into the initial risk reserve w.

Restricting our consideration to the nonlife type of insurance company Lundberg's early researches were thus mainly concerned with finding algebraic and numerical expressions for $F(x, t)$ given by (10), and what we may call the probability of eternal survival of a company with a current risk reserve of w, a probability we will write as $U(w)$. Note particularly that because of the exponential assumption for $A(t)$ the choice of the time origin for $F(x, t)$ and $U(w)$ could be at the occurrence of a claim or be made arbitrarily. This assumption was used in all the risk theoretic literature until 0. Lundberg (1940) introduced ideas that led to the negative binomial for $p_n(t)$ and thus implicitly required $F(x, t)$ and $U(w)$ to be written in the case of an arbitrary time origin and, say, $F_0(x, t)$ and $U_0(w)$ in the case that the time origin is contemporaneous with a claim. Of course when $t \to \infty$, as it does with $U(w)$, it may be surmised that the occurrence of a claim at the origin does not affect the probability to be calculated.

The history of attempts to calculate $F(x, t)$ for Poisson and negative binomial $p_n(t)$ is summarized by Cramér (1955, Ch. 4) and an extensive numerical review is found in Bohman and Esscher (1963–64). A similar history of $U(w)$ is in Cramér (1955, Chapter 5) with an indication of how much harder it was to obtain formulas and numerical results for what we write as $U(w, t)$, the probability of survival (at least) to epoch t. The Cramér text is eloquent witness to the importance of asymptotic methods in the approximation of $F(x, t)$ and $U(w, t)$. We may say that the classic period of Risk Theory ended when electronic computers became generally available for the 'exact' calculation of these two functions under the sole restriction that $p_n(t)$ must be invariant for any choice of time origin, this restriction implying that claim occurrence epochs form a so-called stationary point process. In what follows, then, we will show why relation (10) for $F(x, t)$ plays a central part in the numerical calculation of $U(w, t)$, and describe methods of numerically evaluating both these functions.

CHAPTER 2

The Choices for $p_n(t)$ and $B(\cdot)$; the Simplest Model of a Nonlife Company; and the Use of Queueing Techniques

In Chapter 1 we proposed a model for a nonlife insurance company based on two independent probability distributions:

(1) that of T, the time interval between successive claims, with distribution function $A(\cdot)$, and
(2) that of individual claim sizes Y with distribution function $B(\cdot)$.

Both these functions are zero at the origin. Historically $A(\cdot)$ was at first assumed to be of the exponential form

$$A(t) = 1 - e^{-\lambda t} \quad 0 < t < \infty; \lambda > 0 \tag{1}$$

and it was not until Ove Lundberg's thesis (1940) that more general, and, in some cases, more realistic, forms were considered for $p_n(t)$ than the Poisson. Seal (1969, pp. 13–29) reviews the literature on this subject; it would seem that a mixture of Poisson distributions (Kendall and Stuart, 1977, Section 5.13) has been the most successful for $p_n(t)$ but there has not been much variability within risk theory proper.

THE POISSON, NEGATIVE BINOMIAL AND GENERALIZED WARING DISTRIBUTIONS

The Bohman and Esscher (1963–64) paper, for example, was limited to claim occurrence distributions in which $p_n(t)$ was either Poisson, namely

$$p_n(t) = e^{-t} \frac{t^n}{n!} \quad n = 0, 1, 2, \ldots \tag{2}$$

or negative binomial, namely

$$p_n(t) = \binom{h+n-1}{n} \left(\frac{h}{t+h}\right)^h \left(\frac{t}{t+h}\right)^n \quad n = 0, 1, 2, \ldots \tag{3}$$

In both cases the time scale has been chosen so that

$$E\{N(t)\} = t$$

and the negative binomial tends to the Poisson as $h \to \infty$. It is important to note that the lengths of successive intervals between claims under the negative binomial law are not independent of one another (McFadden, 1962). It can be shown that the variance of the negative binomial is $t(1 + t/h)$ and it is seen that this is only substantially greater than the Poisson value t when t is much larger than h. Judging by the Bohman—Esscher choices of h, this parameter rarely has a value less than about 20. We can thus sympathize with Segerdahl (1970) who found it 'disagreeable and somewhat alarming that the increased rapidity in the growth' of the variance of $X(t)$ should 'make itself felt only in a fairly remote future'. Nevertheless the modification we are proposing does not solve this difficulty which may be inherent in realistic distributions for $p_n(t)$.

The negative binomial first occurred as the distribution of the number of repeated accidents suffered by an individual in a given time span (Seal, 1969, Chapter 2) and it is no coincidence that we look for its generalization in accident theory (Irwin, 1968). Suppressing specific reference to the length of time during which the accidents may occur, let us assume that an individual with an accident proneness of ν and a liability λ to have an accident has a probability

$$e^{-\lambda \nu} \frac{(\lambda \nu)^n}{n!}$$

of having n accidents. We suppose that individuals with proneness ν to accident have a continuous liability density

$$\frac{h^h}{\Gamma(h)} e^{-h\lambda} \lambda^{h-1} \qquad 0 < \lambda < \infty, h > 0$$

The probability of an individual with proneness ν, chosen at random, having n accidents is thus

$$\frac{h^h \nu^n}{(h+\nu)^{n+h} \Gamma(h) n!} \int_0^\infty e^{-(h+\nu)\lambda} \{(h+\nu)\lambda\}^{n+h-1} d\{(h+\nu)\lambda\}$$

$$= \frac{\Gamma(n+h)}{\Gamma(h) n!} \left(\frac{h}{h+\nu}\right)^h \left(\frac{\nu}{h+\nu}\right)^n \qquad n = 0, 1, 2, \ldots$$

the negative binomial (3). This distribution is called a 'mixed Poisson with a gamma mixing distribution'. Now suppose that the accident proneness ν has a density

$$\frac{\Gamma(\rho + k)}{\Gamma(\rho)\Gamma(k)} h^{-k} \nu^{k-1} \left(1 + \frac{\nu}{h}\right)^{-(\rho+k)} \qquad k > 0, \rho > 0$$

where ρ and k are given parameters, then the probability that an individual chosen at random will suffer n accidents in the specified time span is

$$\frac{\Gamma(\rho + k)}{\Gamma(\rho)\Gamma(k)} \cdot \frac{\Gamma(h + n)}{\Gamma(h)n!} \int_0^\infty \left(\frac{v}{h}\right)^{n+k-1} \left(\frac{h}{h+v}\right)^{\rho+k+h+n} d\left(\frac{v}{h}\right)$$

$$= \frac{\Gamma(\rho + k)}{\Gamma(\rho)\Gamma(k)} \cdot \frac{\Gamma(h + n)}{\Gamma(h)n!} \int_0^1 u^{k+n-1}(1 - u)^{\rho+h-1}du \quad \text{with } u = \frac{v}{h + v}$$

$$= \frac{\Gamma(\rho + k)\Gamma(\rho + h)}{\Gamma(\rho)\Gamma(\rho + h + k)} \cdot \frac{1}{n!} \cdot \frac{\Gamma(h + n)\Gamma(k + n)}{\Gamma(h)\Gamma(k)} \cdot \frac{\Gamma(\rho + h + k)}{\Gamma(\rho + h + k + n)} \quad n = 0, 1, 2, \ldots$$

Writing

$$\frac{\Gamma(a + n)}{\Gamma(a)} = a(a + 1) \ldots (a + n - 1) \equiv (a)_n$$

the probability generating function of what Irwin has called the generalized Waring distribution is

$$\frac{\Gamma(\rho + k)\Gamma(\rho + h)}{\Gamma(\rho)\Gamma(\rho + h + k)} \sum_{n=0}^\infty \frac{(h)_n(k)_n}{(\rho + h + k)_n} \frac{z^n}{n!} = \frac{\Gamma(\rho + k)\Gamma(\rho + h)}{\Gamma(\rho)\Gamma(\rho + h + k)} {}_2F_1(h, k; \rho + h + k; z)$$

$$(4)$$

in the notation of the Gaussian hypergeometric function (Luke, 1975). The mean of this distribution is

$$\frac{hk}{\rho - 1} \quad (\rho > 1)$$

and its variance is

$$\frac{hk(\rho + h - 1)(\rho + k - 1)}{(\rho - 1)^2(\rho - 2)} \quad (\rho > 2)$$

(Irwin, 1975).

If we consider that the accident occurrences should form a stationary point process (McFadden, 1962) the probability of no accidents in a given interval of length t is

$$p_0(t) = 1 - G_1(t) = \frac{\Gamma(\rho + k)\Gamma(\rho + h)}{\Gamma(\rho)\Gamma(\rho + k + h)}$$

where t is now proportionate to $hk/(\rho - 1)$ and $G_1(\cdot)$ is the distribution function of the length of the interval between an arbitrary (random) epoch and the first accident that occurs thereafter. More generally we can obtain recursively (McFadden, 1962)

$$G_{n+1}(t) = G_n(t) - p_n(t) \quad n = 1, 2, 3, \ldots$$

where $G_n(\cdot)$ is the distribution function of the length of the interval between the arbitrary epoch and the nth accident following it.

The proportionality of $hk/(\rho - 1)$ to t may be achieved by writing

$$h = at \quad k = bt \quad \text{and} \quad \rho = ct + 1 \tag{5}$$

but a good fit of the generalized Waring distribution to accidents (or claims) occurring in an interval of time $(0, t)$ would have to be maintained in a time interval $(0, 2t)$ and in $(0, 3t)$, etc. Similar remarks apply to the foregoing negative binomial and Poisson parameterizations but numerical vindications have seldom been attempted. In passing it may be noted that the gamma functions preceding the hypergeometric function in (4) can become enormous for large t; substantial cancellation occurs when h or k is an integer.

The foregoing relations imply that the mean of $p_n(t)$ is

$$\frac{ab}{c} t \quad (\text{namely}, t \text{ if } ab = c) \tag{6}$$

and its variance

$$\frac{ab(c + a)(c + b)}{c^2 \left(c - \dfrac{1}{t} \right)} t \tag{7}$$

The negative binomial is a special case of the generalized Waring distribution. By (3) its probability generating function is

$$\left(\frac{h}{t + h} \right)^h \sum_{n=0}^{\infty} \binom{-h}{n} \left(\frac{-t}{t + h} z \right)^n = \left(\frac{h}{t + h} \right)^h \left(1 - \frac{t}{t + h} z \right)^{-h}$$

But (Luke, 1975, Chapter II)

$$_2F_1(-a, b; b; -x) = (1 + x)^a$$

so the foregoing probability generating function is

$$\left(\frac{h}{t + h} \right)^h {}_2F_1 \left(h, b; b; \frac{t}{t + h} z \right) \tag{8}$$

where b is arbitrary and cancels out in the expansion.

As Irwin (1975) points out, when $\rho \to \infty$ and $h \to \infty$ with $1 - p = q = h/(h + \rho)$ constant and $k \neq 0$ finite, the generalized Waring (4) tends to the negative binomial

$$p^k(1 - qz)^{-k}$$

When now $k \to \infty$ and $q \to 0$ with kq remaining finite we have the Poisson distribution $\exp\{kq(z - 1)\}$. The three distributions of numbers of claim occurrences are thus closely related. However the generalized Waring is not a mixed Poisson distribution as the negative binomial is. This will have important consequences in Chapter 4.

Table 2.1. *Comparison of generalized Waring and negative binomial distributions with same means t and variances $15t^2/(8t - 1)$ (five decimal places)*

$t =$	2		5		10	
n	Waring	Negative binomial ($h = 2$)	Waring	Negative binomial	Waring	Negative binomial
0	23663	25000	2589	2895	65	80
5	4422	4688	12766	12560	6004	5975
10	278	269	2910	3023	9120	9047
15	22	12	349	337	3826	3910
20	2	1	35	26	867	873
25	–	–	3	2	141	129
30			–	–	19	14
35					2	1
40					–	–

Table 2.2. *Comparison of generalized Waring and negative binomial distributions with same means t and variances $4t^2/(t - 1)$ (five decimal places)*

$t =$	2		5		10	
n	Waring	Negative binomial	Waring	Negative binomial	Waring	Negative binomial
0	40000	55205	8392	13375	615	1316
5	3117	2790	8593	7449	7592	6942
10	604	881	2572	2861	6191	5805
15	189	340	813	1032	3048	3237
20	77	142	292	363	1309	1500
25	37	62	118	125	548	625
30	20	28	52	43	234	243
35	12	13	25	15	103	90
40	7	6	13	5	47	32
45	5	3	7	2	22	11
50	3	1	4	1	11	4
55	2	1	2	–	6	1
60	2	–	1	–	3	–
65	1	–	1	–	2	–
70	1	–	1	–	1	–
75	1	–	–	–	1	–
80	1	–			–	–
85	–	–				

The generalized Waring distribution has a very long tail when ρ is fairly small as can be guessed from the fact that its mean is infinite when $\rho \leqslant 1$ and its variance is infinite when $\rho \leqslant 2$. Irwin (1975), for example, calculates (in his Table 3) that when $\rho = 4.5$ and $h = k = 18$ the upper 5% point of the distributon is at $n = 215$ and the 1% point at $n = 353$. Only two actual sets of data were fitted by Irwin in the cited papers and one of these led to an infinite variance; in both k and h were fairly small numbers.

It is interesting to compare the generalized Waring distribution with the negative binomial with the same mean and variance. Table 2.1 shows such a comparison with $a = 4$, $b = 2$ and $c = 8$ in (5). When $t = 1$ these are broadly the parameters of one of Irwin's fitted distributions. The lengthening of the tail of the Waring in comparison with the negative binomial is fairly small and discrimination between the two laws would require a vast number of data. On the other hand when $a = b = c = 1$ Table 2.2 shows a clear distinction between the two laws especially for small t. Note that in both these tables ab/c is unity so that the mean of the distribution is t.

DISTRIBUTIONS USED FOR $B(\cdot)$

The forms that have been used for $B(\cdot)$ are theoretically more varied (Seal, 1969, pp. 29–31). A characteristic feature of this distribution is its long tail and has encouraged the use of the Pareto distribution which must be truncated at a large Y-value (as in Cramér (1955, p. 43)) if a Laplace transform (see Chapter 3) is to be used. Benktander (1970) has illustrated the successful use of two distributions specially developed for larger claim amounts, viz.

$$B(x) = 1 - cx^{a-1-b \ln x}(a + 2b \ln x)$$

and

$$B(x) = 1 - cax^{b-1} \exp(-ax^b/b)$$

A more familiar choice is the lognormal, namely the distribution of Y which becomes Normal on using the transformation $Z = \log Y$. Seal (1978) has suggested that the mathematical difficulties associated with this distribution, the principal one of which is that it has no explicit Laplace transform, would be dissipated by the use of the rather similar inverse normal distribution for $B(\cdot)$ (Johnson and Kotz, 1970). Among the lognormal distributions fitted to insurance claim amount distributions and cited by Seal (1969, p. 30) we took 45 and calculated $\gamma_1 = \alpha_3 = \mu_3 \mu_2^{3/2}$ from the values of a and b used in the linear transformation $a \ln X + b$. This ratio is an index of skewness of the distribution. Since the mean (μ) and variance (μ^3/λ) of the inverse normal with density

$$b(x) = \left(\frac{\lambda}{2\pi x^3}\right)^{1/2} \exp\left[-\frac{\lambda(x-\mu)^2}{2\mu^2 x}\right] \qquad x > 0, \mu > 0, \lambda > 0$$

Table 2.3.

Author and type of data	Number of distributions fitted	γ_1 for each fitted lognormal	γ_1 for corresponding inverse normal
Amoroso (1934): accident and liability insurance claims	14	1.246	1.184
		1.126	1.080
		1.206	1.149
		1.476	1.379
		1.382	1.301
		1.399	1.315
		1.441	1.350
		0.663	0.652
		0.506	0.501
		0.522	0.516
		0.510	0.505
		0.539	0.534
		0.346	0.345
		0.439	0.436
Amoroso (1942): sickness durations	5	0.759	0.744
		0.748	0.733
		0.704	0.691
		0.751	0.736
		0.737	0.723
Cannella (1963): pharmaceutical drug costs	2	0.355	0.354
		0.369	0.367
Ferrara (1971): fire insurance claims	9	41815.0	104.04
		5461.8	52.662
		595.0	24.876
		3194.7	43.980
		1769.5	36.038
		442156.[a]	228.51
		970.0	29.394
		1006.7	29.768
		49168.8	109.82
Bühlmann and Hartmann (1956): industrial accidents in excess of 141 Francs	1	6.122	3.909
Bailey (1942–43): automobile claims	1	3.644	3.627
Dropkin (1966): workmen's compensation	5	0.374	0.372
		0.379	0.377
		0.371	0.369
		0.405	0.403
		0.372	0.370

Table 2.3. (Continued)

Author and type of data	Number of distributions fitted	γ_1 for each fitted lognormal	γ_1 for corresponding inverse normal
Benckert (1962):	8	466.53	22.881
fire, accident and motor		105.55	13.544
insurance claims		11824.0	68.214
(truncated)		5680.0	53.359
		9.258	4.900
		8.459	4.675
		1439.0	33.604
		759.69	27.045

[a]This enormous γ_1 is based on the estimated lognormal parameters. Judging by Ferrara's Tableau 1 the 'observed' γ_1 was about 7.6.

can be equated to the corresponding values of the lognormal, γ_1 for the inverse normal (namely $3\sqrt{(\mu/\lambda)}$) can be compared with the lognormal value to see whether the two distributions are similar with respect to their skewnesses. Table 2.3 makes this comparison for the 45 distributions. We observe that the pairs of γ_1-values of Ferrara's nine distributions and Benckert's eight are widely different and that Bühlmann and Hartmann's pair are also dissimilar; the remaining 27 pairs of γ_1-values show good agreement. Except for fire insurance and occasionally in other branches the inverse normal may well be used instead of the lognormal.

We mention that $b(\cdot)$ can sometimes be split into two (or more) parts each of which has its own Laplace transform, the sum being the transform of $b(\cdot)$. The long tailed lognormal distributions of Table 2.3 could, perhaps, be analysed in this manner.

Methods of calculating $F(x, t)$ and $U(w, t)$ for the foregoing 'practical' forms of $p_n(t)$ and $B(\cdot)$ will be developed in Chapter 4. In the meantime we will consider the unrealistic assumption that

$$B(y) = 1 - e^{-\mu y} \quad 0 < y < \infty; \mu > 0 \tag{9}$$

coupled with (1) for $A(\cdot)$. This is one of two families for $B(\cdot)$ – the other one being the unit atom or spike of probability at a specified value of Y – for which explicit results are available for $U(w, t)$ when $A(t)$ is given by (1).

QUEUEING MODELS

What is extraordinary is that the model of Chapter 1 is *exactly* the same as that developed by Erlang (1909) for telephone calls on a single line and later adopted generally for queues with a single server who attends to customers in their order of arrival (Kendall, 1951). Like Lundberg before him Erlang started with an exponential law for $A(\cdot)$, which he assumed to be the distribution of intervals between telephone calls, and demonstrated that this implied a Poisson distribution for the number of independent telephone calls in a given period. While his first 'holding' (or service) time distribution $B(\cdot)$ was the unit atom of probability at a specified time, in 1917 he used the form (9). Kendall has called this the $M/M/1$ queue, the two letters (Markov) indicating an exponential distribution for (a) inter-customer arrival intervals, and (b) customer service times, respectively, and the unit showing that a single server is involved. This model was later used by Lundberg and we may refer to it as the Poisson/exponential case, the first word indicating the form used for $p_n(t)$ and the second being the probability distribution of individual claims.

Now although the models are identical for nonlife insurance companies and for queues with a single server the questions asked of the applied mathematician are completely different. While our $X(t)$, the aggregate claims payable through epoch t, corresponds exactly to the notional service load that has been assumed by the server by epoch t if there is no queue at $t = 0$ this hypothetical quantity – for some of the service times may not even have commenced – is not of much interest to the congestion engineer. His problems are more usually: (i) what is the probability distribution of the number in the queue at epoch t, and (ii) what is the probability distribution of the (virtual) waiting time of a customer who arrives at epoch t. It is surprising that, provided the intervals between claims (customer arrivals at the queue) are independent – thus ruling out two of the three distributions we have proposed for $p_n(t)$ – the distribution function of the virtual waiting time W is the same as the survival probability in risk theory when $W = w$ (see, e.g. Seal, 1972b). We may thus expect to be able to use some of the numerical results of queueing theory in our efforts to obtain $U(w, t)$.

$U(w, t)$ FOR THE $M/M/1$ CASE

Many textbooks on queueing theory (e.g. Saaty, 1961 (4–24); Takács, 1962, p. 23 with misprint; Prabhu, 1965 (1.46); Cohen, 1969 (4.32); Gross and Harris, 1974 (2.57)) derive an explicit formula for $q_n(t)$, the probability that there are n customers in the queue at epoch t including the customer being served (if any), $n = 0, 1, 2, 3, \ldots$, in the $M/M/1$ case. It is assumed that when the time scale starts there are no customers at the server. The formula is

$$q_n(t) = e^{-(\lambda+\mu)t} \left[\left(\frac{\lambda}{\mu}\right)^{k/2} I_n(2t\sqrt{\lambda\mu}) + \left(\frac{\lambda}{\mu}\right)^{(n-1)/2} I_{n+1}(2t\sqrt{\lambda\mu}) \right]$$

$$+ \left(1 - \frac{\lambda}{\mu}\right)\left(\frac{\lambda}{\mu}\right)^n \left[1 - e^{-(\lambda+\mu)t} \sum_{k=0}^{\infty} \frac{(\lambda t)^k}{k!} \sum_{l=0}^{n+k+1} \frac{(\mu t)^l}{l!} \right] \tag{10}$$

where $I_n(\cdot)$ is a modified Bessel function given by

$$I_n(y) = \sum_{j=0}^{\infty} \frac{(y/2)^{n+2j}}{j!(n+j)!} \quad n = 0, 1, 2, \ldots \tag{11}$$

Now if there are n customers in the queue when a new customer arrives at epoch t this new customer must wait for n customers' services to be completed, the customer in service having a service probability distribution the same as that of the unattended customers because of (9). Hence

$$\Pr\{W \leqslant w \mid t\} = U(w, t) = \sum_{n=0}^{\infty} q_n(t) B^{n*}(w) \tag{12}$$

where it is well-known for the exponential distribution that the distribution function of the sum of n identical independent random variables is

$$B^{n*}(w) = \frac{\mu^n}{\Gamma(n)} \int_0^w e^{-\mu x} x^{n-1} dx \equiv P(n, \mu w) \tag{13}$$

This incomplete gamma function ratio may be calculated by reference to Khamis's (1965) tables, or directly by means of his relation (11), namely

$$P(n, x) = \frac{x^n e^{-x}}{\Gamma(n)} \sum_{j=0}^{\infty} \frac{x^j}{n(n+1)\cdots(n+j)} \tag{14}$$

which he recommends be replaced by its asymptotic value when $x \geqslant 280$.

The five queueing textbooks cited above do not provide any tables of numerical values of $q_n(t)$ or $U(w, t)$ or of the distribution function of the waiting time of the nth arrival at the queue, $W_n(w)$ say, in this 'simple' $M/M/1$ case. Nor are there any published articles with such tables to be found in Neuts's excellent 516-item annotated bibliography (1976). It was thus of interest to calculate some values of $U(w, t)$ by (10) and (12) to compare them with the values computed by Arfwedson's risk theoretic formula derived below.

We have already mentioned that it is customary to measure insurance company claim amounts in units of the mean claim so that

$$E(Y) = 1 = \mu^{-1} = \mu$$

And since F. Lundberg wrote his thesis it has been usual to write $\lambda = 1$ so that the expected number of claims in an interval of length t is t itself. However, corresponding to risk theory's risk-loaded premium rate $1 + \eta$ we have the reciprocal of queueing theory's traffic intensity, namely μ/λ (Seal, 1972b). Thus throughout relation (10) we put $\lambda = 1$ and $\mu = 1 + \eta$ but in (12) $B(\cdot)$, being solely concerned with claim amounts (service times), has $\mu = 1$.

The case $t = 10$ (10 claims 'expected') and $\eta = 0.1$ (a 10% risk-loading) seems adequate illustration of the calculation of $U(w, t)$ for $w = 0, 1, 2, \ldots 10$, namely initial risk reserves of up to ten times the mean claim amount. The first question is: how many terms are likely to be needed in the summation of relation (12) to produce, say, five correct decimals in $U(w, t)$? For $t = 10$ we 'expect' 10 arrivals at the server (claims) and the probability of a queue length of 20 should be fairly small. We therefore calculated q_n (10) for n up to 20 by:

(1) Calculating I_0 by (11) stopping the summation when the last item was 4×10^{-8} or less;
(2) Using IBM's SSP subroutine BESI — which is using (11) with 31 terms — with its 'tolerance' changed from 10^{-6} to 10^{-7} for I_1 and I_2;
(3) Employing the recursion formula

$$I_n(y) = I_{n-2}(y) - \frac{2(n-1)}{y} I_{n-1}(y)$$

for $n = 3, 4, \ldots 21$;
(4) Utilizing the first 31 terms of the infinite sum in (10), the value of the last term decreasing rather slowly from 1.4×10^{-8} at $n = 1$ to 2.3×10^{-9} at $n = 20$.

The resulting series for $q_n(10)$ decreased from 0.2 at $n = 0$ to 7×10^{-6} at $n = 20$. It was guessed that a 21-term sum in (12) should be adequate and, after confirming from Khamis (1965) that if the last term in (14) were chosen to be not greater than 4×10^{-8} the result would be a seven decimal $P(n, x)$ with occasional unit last place errors, $P(20, w)$ was found to range from 1.5×10^{-19} for $w = 1$ up to 3.5×10^{-3} for $w = 10$.

The resulting values of $U(w, 10)$, $w = 0, 1, 2, \ldots 10$, were:

    0.21457   0.38742   0.53087   0.64690   0.73857   0.80943

    0.86312   0.90305   0.93223   0.95322   0.96810

the whole job being done in less than six seconds of computation on a CDC 6500.

We have described the above calculations in some detail because nearly all the techniques that follow involve numerical quadratures, frequently over infinite ranges. And with the best will in the world we cannot be certain that the resulting value of the integral has anything like its first five significant figures correct. On the contrary, in the foregoing computations we were always within an ace of extending our results to a further figure or two. We would be surprised if we had not achieved five decimal accuracy in $U(w, t)$ — although many will think this is excessive!

ARFWEDSON'S FORMULA FOR $U(w, t)$

Consider $U(0, t)$, the probability of survival through the interval $(0, t)$ given that the risk business started the interval with a zero risk reserve. Then if the aggregate claims in the interval amount to $z < \pi_1 t = (1 + \eta)t$, the probability of which is $f(z, t)dz$, the probability that $X(\tau)$, $0 \leqslant \tau < t$, has never exceeded $\pi_1 \tau$ is

Table 2.4

$U(w, t)$, $\eta = 0.1$

t	w = 0	1	2	3	4	5	6	7	8	9	10
1	0.53660	0.76194	0.88029	0.94085	0.97121	0.98616	0.99342	0.99690	0.99855	0.99933	0.99969
2	0.40714	0.64543	0.79433	0.88367	0.93560	0.96499	0.98127	0.99012	0.99486	0.99735	0.99865
3	0.34479	0.57402	0.73154	0.83524	0.90118	0.94191	0.96645	0.98093	0.98932	0.99409	0.99677
4	0.30669	0.52472	0.68359	0.79471	0.86979	0.91907	0.95061	0.97035	0.98246	0.98977	0.99410
5	0.28040	0.48811	0.64558	0.76049	0.84164	0.89734	0.93464	0.95906	0.97474	0.98463	0.99077
6	0.26088	0.45957	0.61455	0.73125	0.81646	0.87701	0.91901	0.94752	0.96649	0.97890	0.98688
7	0.24566	0.43653	0.58863	0.70596	0.79389	0.85812	0.90397	0.93600	0.95797	0.97277	0.98258
8	0.23337	0.41745	0.56658	0.68384	0.77359	0.84064	0.88962	0.92469	0.94934	0.96637	0.97796
9	0.22319	0.40130	0.54753	0.66430	0.75524	0.82444	0.87601	0.91369	0.94074	0.95983	0.97311
10	0.21457	0.38742	0.53087	0.64690	0.73857	0.80943	0.86312	0.90305	0.93224	0.95323	0.96810
20	0.16816	0.30939	0.43267	0.53879	0.62889	0.70438	0.76683	0.81785	0.85904	0.89191	0.91785
30	0.14798	0.27393	0.38578	0.48419	0.57000	0.64413	0.70760	0.76147	0.80678	0.84458	0.87584
40	0.13621	0.25289	0.35738	0.45033	0.53247	0.60458	0.66744	0.72188	0.76871	0.80872	0.84269
50	0.12836	0.23872	0.33804	0.42696	0.50618	0.57639	0.63827	0.69253	0.73985	0.78090	0.81631

t	w = 0	11	22	33	44	55	66	77	88	99	110
50	0.12836	0.84671	0.98438	0.99904	0.99996	1.	1.	1.	1.	1.	1.
100	0.11001	0.77244	0.95621	0.99373	0.99933	0.99994	1.	1.	1.	1.	1.
150	0.10282	0.73611	0.93517	0.98695	0.99786	0.99971	0.99997	1.	1.	1.	1.
200	0.09902	0.71512	0.92050	0.98080	0.99602	0.99929	0.99989	0.99998	0.99999	1.	1.
400	0.09343	0.68177	0.89287	0.96584	0.98979	0.99716	0.99927	0.99982	0.99994	0.99998	1.
600	0.09191	0.67215	0.88372	0.95977	0.98652	0.99565	0.99865	0.99960	0.99986	0.99996	0.99999
800	0.09136	0.66853	0.88009	0.95715	0.98494	0.99482	0.99826	0.99943	0.99980	0.99993	0.99998
1000	0.09112	0.66698	0.87848	0.95593	0.98416	0.99437	0.99802	0.99932	0.99976	0.99991	0.99997
1500	0.09095	0.66582	0.87725	0.95496	0.98350	0.99397	0.99780	0.99920	0.99970	0.99989	0.99996
2000	0.09092	0.66562	0.87702	0.95478	0.98337	0.99387	0.99773	0.99914	0.99966	0.99985	0.99993
∞	0.09091	0.66556	0.87697	0.95474	0.98335	0.99387	0.99775	0.99917	0.99970	0.99989	0.99996

Table 2.5

$U(w, t), \eta = 0.0$

t	$w = 0$	1	2	3	4	5	6	7	8	9	10
1	0.52378	0.75406	0.87580	0.93842	0.96993	0.98551	0.99309	0.99674	0.99848	0.99929	0.99967
2	0.38575	0.62804	0.78207	0.87572	0.93072	0.96212	0.97963	0.98921	0.99436	0.99708	0.99851
3	0.31871	0.54911	0.71164	0.82083	0.89140	0.93557	0.96249	0.97853	0.98789	0.99327	0.99630
4	0.27757	0.49389	0.65684	0.77381	0.85457	0.90852	0.94357	0.96580	0.97960	0.98802	0.99304
5	0.24910	0.45252	0.61280	0.73344	0.82085	0.88216	0.92399	0.95183	0.96996	0.98154	0.98881
6	0.22789	0.42005	0.57647	0.69846	0.79019	0.85703	0.90442	0.93721	0.95941	0.97414	0.98376
7	0.21131	0.39368	0.54586	0.66786	0.76234	0.83332	0.88524	0.92233	0.94825	0.96603	0.97800
8	0.19789	0.37172	0.51963	0.64085	0.73699	0.81105	0.86666	0.90745	0.93675	0.95740	0.97169
9	0.18674	0.35307	0.49683	0.61680	0.71384	0.79020	0.84879	0.89276	0.92508	0.94840	0.96493
10	0.17729	0.33697	0.47678	0.59522	0.69263	0.77066	0.83168	0.87837	0.91338	0.93916	0.95782
20	0.12576	0.24501	0.35614	0.45764	0.54860	0.62869	0.69804	0.75713	0.80675	0.84783	0.88137
30	0.10279	0.20198	0.29653	0.38535	0.46767	0.54295	0.61092	0.67157	0.72505	0.77168	0.81191
40	0.08907	0.17577	0.25939	0.33912	0.41433	0.48454	0.54942	0.60878	0.66260	0.71093	0.75395
50	0.07969	0.15768	0.23343	0.30632	0.37584	0.44158	0.50321	0.56053	0.61341	0.66181	0.70578

t	$w = 0$	11	22	33	44	55	66	77	88	99	110
50	0.07969	0.74543	0.96330	0.99701	0.99985	1.	1.	1.	1.	1.	1.
100	0.05638	0.59118	0.87760	0.97439	0.99617	0.99958	0.99997	1.	1.	1.	1.
150	0.04605	0.50370	0.80017	0.93780	0.98492	0.99712	0.99956	0.99995	1.	1.	1.
200	0.03988	0.44602	0.73716	0.89789	0.96746	0.99145	0.99813	0.99966	0.99995	0.99999	1.
400	0.02821	0.32649	0.57755	0.76124	0.87868	0.94462	0.97728	0.99161	0.99721	0.99916	0.99977
600	0.02303	0.26976	0.48941	0.66709	0.79802	0.88612	0.94037	0.97100	0.98690	0.99450	0.99786
800	0.01995	0.23503	0.43204	0.59985	0.73294	0.83137	0.89935	0.94323	0.96975	0.98477	0.99275
1000	0.01784	0.21098	0.39098	0.54918	0.68043	0.78330	0.85956	0.91305	0.94859	0.97098	0.98436
1500	0.01457	0.17310	0.32433	0.46300	0.58528	0.68902	0.77373	0.84033	0.89077	0.92758	0.95348
2000	0.01262	0.15028	0.28314	0.40761	0.52083	0.62083	0.70663	0.77815	0.83608	0.88171	0.91663

always zero for finite w

8

$1 - z/\{(1 + \eta)t\}$ by the so-called ballot theorem. [The result is equivalent to (4.6) which is proved in Chapter 4.]

$$U(0, t) = \int_0^{(1 + \eta)t} \left\{ 1 - \frac{z}{(1 + \eta)t} \right\} f(z, t)dz$$

$$= F(\overline{1 + \eta} \cdot t, t) - \frac{1 + \eta}{t} \int_0^t zf(\overline{1 + \eta} \cdot z, t)dz \tag{15}$$

Now in the particular Poisson/exponential case relation (1.8) becomes ($\lambda = \mu = 1$)

$$f(x, t) = \sum_{n=1}^{\infty} e^{-t} \frac{t^n}{n!} \frac{1}{\Gamma(n)} e^{-x} x^{n-1} \quad \text{by (13)}$$

$$= \frac{t}{x} \sum_{n=1}^{\infty} e^{-x} \frac{x^n}{n!} \frac{1}{\Gamma(n)} e^{-t} t^{n-1}$$

$$= \frac{t}{x} f(t, x)$$

and in this special case (15) becomes

$$U(0, t) = F(\overline{1 + \eta} \cdot t, t) - (1 + \eta) \int_0^t e^{(t-z)\eta} f(\overline{1 + \eta} \cdot t, z)dz$$

The monetary variable on the right-hand side is now constant and we may add w to the initial risk reserve of zero to get Arfwedson's (1950) formula

$$U(w, t) = F(w + \overline{1 + \eta} \cdot t, t) - (1 + \eta) \int_0^t e^{(t-z)\eta} f(w + \overline{1 + \eta} \cdot t, z)dz \tag{16}$$

where F and f may be written in terms of modified Bessel functions I_1 by means of (11).

Seal (1972a) describes the calculation of $U(w, t)$ for $\eta = 0.1$ and $\eta = 0.0$ by means of 128-panel repeated trapezoidal quadrature and his results are reproduced as Tables 2.4 and 2.5. On comparing the line for $t = 10$ in Table 2.4 with the values of $U(w, 10)$ obtained above by queueing theory formulas we see that the quadrature has produced five decimal accuracy except for $w = 8$ and 9 where the final decimal may be a unit in error. These tables will be found very useful as 'controls' in the verification of new formulas proposed for the exact or approximate calculation of $U(w, t)$ in the general case.

SURVIVAL THROUGH THE nth CLAIM

Although we have concentrated our attention on $U(w, t)$, the probability of insurance company survival to epoch t, the point of time by which t claims have been 'expected', it would be just as meaningful to ask for $W_n(w)$, the probability of survival to the epoch at which the nth claim occurs. These two probabilities are, presumably, of similar size when n is equated to t. This new probability $W_n(w)$ was considered for the first time by Beard (1971) in the Poisson/exponential case but the corresponding distribution function of waiting times in queueing theory goes back to Pollaczek's work in the nineteen thirties. Because a simple computer program is readily available elsewhere for the $M/M/1$ case let us argue in queueing theory terms.

Write q_{nj} for the probability that there are j customers in the system $-j-1$ actually queueing and one being served $-$ just after the arrival of the nth customer, and f_k for the probability that there are k services completed between the arrival of any two customers ($k = 0, 1, 2, \ldots$). In the $M/M/1$ case (reintroducing general λ and μ)

$$f_k = \int_0^\infty (\lambda e^{-\lambda t}) \left(e^{-\mu t} \frac{(\mu t)^k}{k!} \right) dt \tag{17}$$

the first factor in the integrand being the density of an interval t between two arrivals, and the second being the Poisson probability $p_k(t)$. The integral simplifies so that

$$f_k = \frac{\lambda \mu^k}{(\lambda + \mu)^{k+1}} \quad k = 0, 1, 2, \ldots \tag{18}$$

In the interval between two arrivals the queue size:

(i) goes from $j - 1$ to j if no service is completed (probability f_0);
(ii) remains at j if one service is completed (probability f_1);
(iii) goes from j to $j - k + 1$ if k services are completed (probability f_k).

Hence we have the recursion formula

$$q_{n+1,j} = \sum_{i=j-1}^{\infty} q_{ni} f_{i-j+1} \quad j = 1, 2, 3, \ldots \tag{19}$$

and to obtain $q_{n+1,0}$ we have

$$\sum_{j=0}^{\infty} q_{n+1,j} = 1$$

Finally, analogously to (12),

$$W_n(w) = \sum_{k=0}^{\infty} q_{n,k} B^{k*}(w) \tag{20}$$

where $B^{k*}(\cdot)$ is obtained from (13) with, in our case, $\mu = 1$.

Table 2.6

$W_n(w)$, $\eta = 0.1$

n	w = 0	1	2	3	4	5	6	7	8	9	10
1	0.52381	0.82482	0.93555	0.97629	0.99128	0.99679	0.99882	0.99957	0.99984	0.99994	0.99998
2	0.40503	0.69770	0.85810	0.93651	0.97249	0.98835	0.99515	0.99801	0.99919	0.99967	0.99987
3	0.34578	0.61443	0.79024	0.89247	0.94730	0.97505	0.98851	0.99482	0.99771	0.99900	0.99957
4	0.30883	0.55687	0.73500	0.85047	0.91957	0.95840	0.97917	0.98985	0.99517	0.99774	0.99896
5	0.28302	0.51461	0.69034	0.81268	0.89182	0.93997	0.96782	0.98326	0.99151	0.99579	0.99795
6	0.26371	0.48206	0.65379	0.77935	0.86535	0.92096	0.95518	0.97534	0.98680	0.99310	0.99647
7	0.24857	0.45607	0.62338	0.75012	0.84070	0.90212	0.94184	0.96647	0.98120	0.98971	0.99450
8	0.23630	0.43473	0.59766	0.72440	0.81801	0.88390	0.92827	0.95697	0.97488	0.98569	0.99204
9	0.22610	0.41681	0.57560	0.70167	0.79722	0.86653	0.91477	0.94710	0.96803	0.98114	0.98913
10	0.21744	0.40150	0.55644	0.68145	0.77819	0.85010	0.90156	0.93708	0.96080	0.97616	0.98582
20	0.17052	0.31702	0.44618	0.55793	0.65276	0.73165	0.79598	0.84741	0.88773	0.91871	0.94207
30	0.14996	0.27939	0.39510	0.49739	0.58673	0.66381	0.72948	0.78472	0.83057	0.86815	0.89854
40	0.13793	0.25723	0.36459	0.46045	0.54534	0.61987	0.68472	0.74063	0.78839	0.82880	0.86266
50	0.12988	0.24236	0.34396	0.43521	0.51665	0.58887	0.65248	0.70812	0.75645	0.79812	0.83377

A FORTRAN computer program for q_{nk} is the first program in Appendix A of Bagchi and Templeton (1972) and we used this with $\lambda = 1, \mu = 1.1$ and the routine for relation (13) already discussed to produce $W_n(w)$, $n = 10$, $w = 0, 1, 2, \ldots 10$ using 21 terms of (20) in four seconds on a CDC 6500. The values of $W_{10}(w)$ were:

| 0.21744 | 0.40150 | 0.55644 | 0.68145 | 0.77819 | 0.85010 |
| 0.90156 | 0.93708 | 0.96080 | 0.97616 | 0.98582 |

We mention that the Bagchi–Templeton program for q_{nk} assumes an upper limit to the queue size of $K - 1$ which we equated to 50. Even for $n = 21$ all values of q_{nk} were zero to five decimal places for $k \geqslant 20$, indicating that the 'waiting room' was not yet curbing customer arrivals. The Bagchi–Templeton program was intended for an even more general situation than $M/M/1$ with a waiting room.

Cohen (1969) provides a direct series expansion for $W_n(w)$ in the simple $M/M/1$ case and Seal (1972a) has adapted it for computer calculations to provide Table 2.6 $(\eta = 0.1)$. We note from the line $n = 10$ of this table that the foregoing Bagchi–Templeton results are correct to five decimal places.

VALE TO QUEUEING TECHNIQUES

The calculations of queue length in (10) and (19) seem to promise well for more general situations. Unfortunately in the case $M/G/1$, where G stands for 'general', a 'memoryless' Markov chain only exists for values of t at which successive customers' services are completed (Kendall, 1953) and $q_n(t)$ can only be calculated at these epochs which do not seem to have any relevance for risk theoretic models. On the other hand when arrivals are occurring independently and services are exponential, summarized as $GI/M/1$, successive customer arrival (claim occurrence) epochs form a Markov chain and $q_n(t)$ can be calculated (Kendall, 1951). The exponential assumption for claim sizes is rarely appropriate and since no more general formulas are available for $q_n(t)$ we regretfully say good-bye to queue length distributions.

CHAPTER 3

A Computational Accessory – The Laplace Transform

Relation (1.10) for the distribution function of $X(t)$, the aggregate claims in $(0, t)$, was

$$F(x, t) = \sum_{n=0}^{\infty} p_n(t) B^{n*}(x) \tag{1}$$

where $B^{n*}(\cdot)$ is the distribution function of the aggregate claim amounts stemming from n claims. The resulting computational question is at once obvious: suppose we have graduated the frequency distribution of claim amounts $b(\cdot)$ suffered during a certain number of years by a nonlife insurance company, and suppose we have been able to represent our results by a mathematical formula; how do we find the density or distribution function of the sum of n such independent claims?

DE MOIVRE'S LEMMA

If the distribution of individual claim amounts were discrete with a fixed increment h so that, for example, the probability of a claim size equal to jh ($j = 1, 2, 3, \ldots m$) could be written as b_j, the probability of the sum of n individual claims is precisely that of De Moivre's (1738) lemma in his Problem III with $b_j = 1/f$ where f is the number of faces in each of his dice, namely:

'To find how many Chances there are upon any number of Dice, each of them of the same number of Faces, to throw any given number of points.'

De Moivre solved this by introducing the probability generating function

$$G(z) = b_0 z^0 + b_1 z^1 + b_2 z^2 + \ldots + b_m z^m$$

where in his case $b_0 = 0$, $b_j = 1/f$, all $j \neq 0$, and $m = f$, and said that it was 'very plain' that the probability of the sum, k, of the faces showing on two dice would be given by the coefficient of z^k in $\{G(z)\}^2$, i.e., in

$$(b_0 z^0 + b_1 z^1 + b_2 z^2 + \ldots + b_m z^m)^2 \qquad k = 0, 1, 2, \ldots 2m$$

26

In general, then, the probability that n claims result in an aggregate claim amount of $k(k = n, n + 1, \ldots nm)$ is the coefficient of z^k in $\{G(z)\}^n$. This coefficient has been written b_k^{n*} in (1.9) except that k has, in effect, been shown as $y = hk$ and put in parentheses. The cumulation of these densities provides the distribution function (1).

We have illustrated De Moivre's procedure by means of a computer program entitled DEMOIV using IBM's SSP subroutine PMPY which multiplies two polynomials together. An important feature of the program is the recognition that b_k^{n*} is likely to be effectively zero for k-values near the beginning and the end of the distribution when n is fairly large. This keeps the number of terms in b^{n*} reasonably small in comparison with the theoretical nm. However the search for evanescent B_k^{n*} in the program assumes that the tail values of the basic claim distribution b_j do not increase. The program would have to be modified if there were individual relatively large spikes of probability in the tail.

NUMERICAL ILLUSTRATION

As an example we used the lognormal distribution of metallurgical fire insurance claims provided by Ferrara (1971), namely a random variable $Y_X = 1.07353$ $\log_{10}(X - 70) - 2.433437$ assumed Normally distributed with zero mean and unit variance. We analysed this distribution into 50 discrete probabilities, namely

$$b_j = \Phi(Y_{4000j}) - \Phi(Y_{4000(j-1)}) \quad j = 2, 3, \ldots 49$$

$$b_1 = \Phi(Y_{4000})$$

$$b_0 = 0$$

and, noting the extreme length of the tail with $\Phi(Y_{196,000}) = 0.999418$ and $\Phi(Y_{320,000}) = 0.999746$, 'graduated' the tail into 29 values of 0.0000200 extending through b_{78} with a final value $b_{79} = 0.0000016$ to complete unity. Probabilities from the nth convolution b_k^{n*} with $n = 1$ (the original distribution), 5, 10, 15, 20, 25, 30, 35, 40 are shown in Table 3.1.

Observe that De Moivre's lemma produces b_k^{n*} for all n up to the value where $p_n(t)$ is evanescent and — because the whole distribution is generated — for all k, not only for a given k. Thus with $p_n(t)$ specified the calculation of $f(jh, t)$, with t fixed, takes place for every j when the distribution b^{n*} is obtained for $n = 1, 2, 3, \ldots$ in succession. The program DEMOIV has been adapted to show this procedure for the Poisson

$$p_n(t) = e^{-t} \frac{t^n}{n!} \quad n = 0, 1, 2, \ldots$$

with $t = 20$. Tables of this latter distribution (or independent calculations) show that the fifth decimal place is unaffected when $n > 42$. Nevertheless the probability generating function of b_j was raised through all powers up to the 46th and

Table 3.1. Convolutions of a discrete approximation to a lognormal distribution (densities $\times 10^5$)

k	1	5	10	15	20	25	30	35	40
1	92296	–	–	–	–	–	–	–	–
5	432	66974	–	–	–	–	–	–	–
10	90	1493	44856	–	–	–	–	–	–
15	35	396	3010	30042	–	–	–	–	–
20	18	167	864	4379	20120	–	–	–	–
25	11	87	369	1380	5483	13476	–	–	–
30	7	52	193	604	1918	6265	9025	–	–
35	5	34	114	318	866	2449	6718	6045	–
40	3	23	74	188	460	1150	2947	6866	4048
45	2	17	50	121	273	619	1446	3390	6757
50	2	12	36	82	175	369	794	1747	3760
55	2	10	27	58	118	236	476	980	2041
60	2	10	22	43	84	160	305	593	1174
65	2	10	21	34	62	113	207	382	720
70	2	10	20	31	48	83	146	259	466
75	2	10	20	30	43	64	107	183	316
80	–	10	20	30	41	56	81	133	223
85	–	1	20	30	40	52	69	101	163
90	–	–	5	30	40	51	64	84	123
95	–	–	2	11	40	50	61	76	101
100	–	–	1	4	20	49	60	72	89
105	–	–	–	2	8	29	59	70	84
110	–	–	–	1	4	13	40	69	81
115	–	–	–	1	2	7	19	52	79
120	–	–	–	–	1	4	10	27	64
125	–	–	–	–	1	2	6	15	36
130	–	–	–	–	1	2	4	9	21
135	–	–	–	–	–	1	3	6	13
140	–	–	–	–	–	1	2	4	8
145	–	–	–	–	–	1	1	3	5
150	–	–	–	–	–	–	1	2	4
155	–	–	–	–	–	–	1	1	3
160	–	–	–	–	–	–	1	1	2
165	–	–	–	–	–	–	–	1	1
170	–	–	–	–	–	–	–	1	1
175	–	–	–	–	–	–	–	1	1
180	–	–	–	–	–	–	–	–	1

Table 3.2. $10^5 f(jh, \ 20)$ and $10^5 F(jh, \ 20)$ for Poisson/discrete lognormal $(h = 4000)$

j	$10^5 f$	$10^5 F$
0	—	—
5	4	5
10	327	624
15	2771	8430
20	5821	32425
25	5095	60807
30	2785	79246
35	1320	88356
40	658	92752
45	365	95074
50	222	96430
55	145	97289
60	100	97869
65	72	98280
70	56	98587
75	47	98837
80	43	99058
85	41	99267
90	40	99468
95	35	99655
100	24	99800
105	13	99888
110	7	99934
115	4	99958
120	2	99971
125	1	99980
130	1	99985
135	1	99989

subsequent calculations produced the distribution $f(jh, 20)$ with $h = 4000$ and its cumulation $F(jh, 20)$. The calculation time for this process with the 79-term discrete lognormal' was 17 seconds on a CDC 6500. A snapshot of part of these distributions is given in Table 3.2 and the very long tail of $f(\cdot, 20)$ is evident from $F(135h, 20)$. The distribution function reaches 0.99999 at a value of $X(t) = 173h$, 12.6 standard deviations in excess of the mean ($25.903h$).

INVERTING A GENERATING FUNCTION

It is natural to wonder whether mathematicians have produced an explicit formula for the coefficient of z^k in the expansion of $\{G(z)\}^n$. This was, in fact, supplied by Laplace just 200 years ago (Seal, 1949) and both the result and its derivation are important for us in what follows. To keep the development separate from our numerical calculations relating to risk theory let us write the generating function of a discrete probability distribution $g_j(j = 0, 1, 2, \ldots)$ as

$$G(z) \equiv \sum_{j=0}^{\infty} g_j z^j$$

We now utilize the imaginary $i = \sqrt{(-1)}$ to form the relation

$$e^{ix} = \cos x + i \sin x$$

and write $z = e^{iu}$. Then

$$G(z) = G(e^{iu}) \equiv H(u) = \sum_{j=0}^{\infty} g_j e^{iuj}$$

$$\equiv K(u) + iL(u)$$

We note that

$$H(-u) = K(u) - iL(u)$$
$$= K(-u) + iL(-u)$$

implying that

$$K(u) = K(-u) \text{ and } L(u) = -L(-u).$$

Now consider (j and k both integers)

$$\int_{-\pi}^{\pi} e^{i(j-k)u} du = \int_{-\pi}^{\pi} [\cos\{(j - k)u\} + i \sin\{(j - k)u\}]du$$

$$= \frac{\sin\{(j - k)u\}}{j - k} - i \frac{\cos\{(j - k)u\}}{j - k} \Bigg|_{u=-\pi}^{\pi}$$

$$= \begin{cases} 0 & j \neq k \\ 2\pi & j = k \end{cases} \tag{2}$$

This result can be used in the definition of $H(u)$. We have

$$e^{-iuk} H(u) = \sum_{j=0}^{\infty} g_j e^{i(j-k)u}$$

and on integrating between $-\pi$ and π

$$\int_{-\pi}^{\pi} e^{-iuk} H(u) du = \sum_{j=0}^{\infty} g_j \int_{-\pi}^{\pi} e^{i(j-k)u} du$$

$$= 2\pi g_k$$

Thus

$$g_k = \frac{1}{2\pi} \int_{-\pi}^{\pi} e^{-iuk} H(u) du \tag{3}$$

We leave it to the reader to show that

$$g_k = \frac{1}{\pi} \int_0^\pi [K(u) \cos(uk) + L(u) \sin(uk)]\, du \tag{4}$$

which is free of the imaginary i.

What the foregoing shows is that if we are given a mathematical expression for the generating function of a discrete probability distribution, namely a formula for $G(z) \equiv H(u)$ which could, for example, be the generating function of the nth convolution of a basic discrete distribution, the coefficient of $z^k \equiv e^{iuk}$ in this expression (g_k in the preceding development) can be obtained directly by integrating a function of $H(u)$. The two formulas

$$H(u) = \sum_{j=0}^\infty g_j e^{iuj} \quad \text{and} \quad g_j = \frac{1}{2\pi} \int_{-\pi}^\pi e^{-iuk} H(u)\, du$$

are known as the Fourier transform of g_j and its 'inverse', respectively.

FOURIER RECIPROCAL RELATIONS AND THE LAPLACE TRANSFORM

Although the observation of an insurance company's claim amount experience invariably results in a discrete distribution $\hat{b}_j$, say, which could be 'graduated' into a mathematical form b_j, preference is always shown for a continuous function $b(y)$ to replace the observed $\hat{b}_j$. This rules out the De Moivre procedure based on a discrete probability distribution and to find the distribution of the sum of n claim amounts we form the so-called characteristic function of $b(y)$, namely

$$\int_0^\infty e^{iuy} b(y)\, dy$$

(analogous to $H(u)$), raise it to its nth power and, in effect, find the coefficient of e^{iux} in the result. The question is: Can we 'invert' the nth power of the preceding characteristic function which is the characteristic function of $b^{n*}(y)$? Or, generally, can we 'invert' a given characteristic function and obtain the underlying density function at the point y?

The procedure to effectuate this is essentially similar to the derivation of g_j from $H(u)$ above. Cramér (1945, Section 10.3) shows that if

$$\phi(u) = \int_{-\infty}^\infty e^{iuy} f(y)\, dy$$

then

$$f(y) = \frac{1}{2\pi} \int_{-\infty}^\infty e^{-iuy} \phi(u)\, du$$

This pair of functions is sometimes called the Fourier pair of reciprocal relations.

Since our probability distributions only extend over non-negative values of a random variable it is more natural to replace the characteristic function by what is called a Laplace transform. Thus for the continuous distribution of claim amounts $b(y)$ we have the Laplace transform

$$\beta(s) = \int_0^\infty e^{-sy}b(y)dy \quad s = c + iu \tag{5}$$

which is called a Laplace–Stieltjes transform when written in the form

$$\beta(s) = \int_0^\infty e^{-sy}dB(y) \quad B(0) = 0$$

and can be used for distributions that are partly continuous and partly discrete.

The Fourier pair of reciprocal relations may be extended to the Laplace transform as follows

$$\beta(s) = \beta(c + iu) = \int_0^\infty [b(v)e^{-cv}]e^{-iuv}dv$$

For fixed c, $\beta(s)$, considered as a function of the variable $-u$, is the characteristic function of a variable whose density is $b(v)e^{-cv}$. A Laplace transform is thus equivalent to a family of characteristic functions and its inverse may be obtained from

$$b(v)e^{-cv} = \frac{1}{2\pi} \int_{-\infty}^\infty e^{iuv}\beta(c + iu)du$$

or

$$b(v) = \frac{e^{cv}}{2\pi} \int_{-\infty}^\infty e^{iuv}\beta(c + iu)du \tag{6}$$

In the foregoing we note the conventional use of the negative power of the exponential in the definition of the Laplace transform (5). Because a characteristic function has a positive powered exponential we have to write $s = c - iu$ (which is uncomfortable) or think in terms of $-u$ instead of u. Further, observe that (6) extends to the negative axis of abscissae even though $b(\cdot)$ is only defined as non-zero for positive abscissae. Finally, we may rewrite (6) as

$$b(v) = \frac{1}{2\pi} \int_{-\infty}^\infty e^{sv}\beta(s)du$$

$$= \frac{1}{2\pi i} \int_{c-i\infty}^{c+i\infty} e^{sv}\beta(s)ds \tag{7}$$

This is known as the Bromwich–Mellin inversion formula for a Laplace transform. The real quantity c has to be greater than c_0, the 'abscissa of convergence' of the L.T. of $b(\cdot)$; this means that c is greater than the real parts of the singularities of the L.T. In practice c is usually chosen as zero or, possibly, as a small positive quantity.

INVERSION FORMULAS

The three computational steps to obtain $b^{n*}(\cdot)$ or $B^{n*}(\cdot)$ from $b(\cdot)$ may thus be effected in terms of the characteristic function of Y or of the Laplace transform of $b(\cdot)$. The last step will be to invert the L.T. $\{\beta(s)\}^n$ or, preferably, the L.T. of $f(x, t)$ or $F(x, t)$ by some form of approximate integration. Let us therefore consider the Laplace transform

$$\gamma(s) = \int_0^\infty e^{-sx} g(x) dx \quad s = c + iu \tag{8}$$

and its inverse

$$g(x) = \frac{1}{2\pi i} \int_{c-i\infty}^{c+i\infty} e^{sx} \gamma(s) ds$$

$$= \frac{e^{cx}}{2\pi} \int_{-\infty}^{\infty} e^{iux} \gamma(c + iu) du \tag{9}$$

Now write

$$\gamma(c + iu) = P(u) + iQ(u)$$

so that

$$P(u) = \mathscr{R}\gamma(c + iu) \quad \text{and} \quad Q(u) = \mathscr{I}\gamma(c + iu)$$

It follows that

$$\gamma(c - iu) = P(-u) + iQ(-u) = P(u) - iQ(u)$$

and equating real and imaginary parts

$$P(-u) = P(u) \quad \text{and} \quad Q(-u) = -Q(u)$$

The inversion formula for $g(\cdot)$ is thus

$$g(x) = \frac{e^{cx}}{2\pi} \int_0^\infty \{e^{iux}\gamma(c + iu) + e^{-iux}\gamma(c - iu)\} du$$

$$= \frac{e^{cx}}{\pi} \int_0^\infty \{P(u)\cos ux - Q(u)\sin ux\} du \tag{10}$$

$$\equiv \frac{e^{cx}}{\pi} \{C(x) - S(x)\}$$

where $C(\cdot)$ and $S(\cdot)$ are Fourier cosine and sine transforms of $P(\cdot)$ and $Q(\cdot)$, respectively. There is a rich computational literature on these transforms but before discussing it we notice that $g(-x)$ is defined to be zero for $x > 0$ so that

$$0 = \frac{e^{-cx}}{\pi} \{C(x) + S(x)\}$$

leading to

$$g(x) = \frac{2e^{cx}}{\pi} C(x) \tag{11}$$

The numerical computation of $C(\cdot)$ and $S(\cdot)$ is treated by Davis and Rabinowitz (1975, Sections 3.9, 3.10) and Squire (1970, Sections 4.13, 4.16, 5.5). The two most important difficulties are the infinite range of u in (9) or (10) and the rapidity with which the integrand changes sign for even moderate values of x. Our own limited experience with risk theoretic $P(\cdot)$ and $Q(\cdot)$ is that the upper limit of integration does not have to be enormous before the integral beyond $u = T$, say, is effectively zero. Davis and Rabinowitz (1975) suggest the use of the asymptotic series

$$\int_T^\infty e^{ixu} h(u)\,du \sim -e^{ixT}\left\{ \frac{h(T)}{ix} - \frac{h'(T)}{(ix)^2} + \dots \right\} \tag{12}$$

where $h(u) = \gamma(c + iu)$, to check this. If x is at least a unit and $|h(T)| < 10^{-5}$ we may say that the integral in (9) beyond $u = T$ is essentially zero. This restriction of the infinite range of (9) to a finite span is important to prevent the 'aliasing' that is occurring in (13) below. Following Davis and Rabinowitz (1975, Section 3.9.5.2)

$$g(x) = \frac{e^{cx}}{2\pi} \int_{-\infty}^{\infty} e^{iux} \gamma(c + iu)\,du$$

$$= \frac{e^{cx}}{2\pi} \sum_{k=-\infty}^{\infty} \int_0^T e^{i(u+kT)x} \gamma(c + i \cdot \overline{u + kT})\,du$$

$$= \frac{e^{cx}}{2\pi} \int_0^T e^{iux} \sum_{k=-\infty}^{\infty} e^{ikTx} \gamma(c + i \cdot \overline{u + kT})\,du$$

If now x is chosen as an integral multiple of $1/T$

$$g(x) = \frac{e^{cx}}{2\pi} \int_0^T e^{iux} \sum_{k=-\infty}^{\infty} \gamma(c + i \cdot \overline{u + kT})\,du \tag{13}$$

which is a finite Fourier transform of the sum of an infinity of γ-functions. Supposing that $\gamma(c + i \cdot \overline{u + kT}) = 0$ for $k = \pm 1, \pm 2, \dots$ we have

$$g(x) = \frac{e^{cx}}{2\pi} \int_{-T}^{T} e^{iux} \gamma(c + iu)\,du$$

namely (9) with a finite range of integration and a single function $\gamma(\cdot)$.

NUMERICAL ILLUSTRATION

We are thus left with the integration of a rapidly oscillating function over a finite interval (Davis and Rabinowitz, 1975, Section 2.10). What we would like is an inversion formula that has worked well on a wide range of risk theoretic Laplace (or Fourier) transforms. As a step in this direction we will illustrate some of the recommended methods on the Laplace transforms of $f(x, t)$ in (i) the Poisson/ exponential, and (ii) the Poisson/inverse normal, cases with $t = x = 10, 100, 1000$.

We first find the Laplace transform of $F(x, t)$ when $p_n(t)$ is Poisson with mean t. Write

$$\psi_t(s) \equiv \int_0^\infty e^{-sx} F(x, t)dx = \sum_{n=0}^\infty e^{-t} \frac{t^n}{n!} \int_0^\infty e^{-sx} B^{n*}(x)dx \qquad \text{from (1)}$$

$$= \sum_{n=0}^\infty e^{-t} \frac{t^n}{n!} \left[B^{n*}(x) \frac{e^{-sx}}{-s} \Big|_0^\infty + \frac{1}{s} \int_0^\infty e^{-sx} dB^{n*}(x) \right]$$

$$= \frac{1}{s} \sum_{n=0}^\infty e^{-t} \frac{t^n}{n!} \{\beta(s)\}^n = \frac{1}{s} \exp\{-t + t\beta(s)\}$$

Further

$$\int_0^\infty e^{-sx} f(x, t)dx = e^{-sx} F(x, t) \Big|_0^\infty + s \int_0^\infty e^{-sx} F(x, t)dx$$

$$= -F(0, t) + s\psi_t(s)$$

where $F(0, t) = p_0(t)$ from (1).

The Laplace transforms which we have to invert numerically are thus

$$s\psi_t(s) - p_0(t) = \exp[-t\{1 - \beta(s)\}] - \exp(-t) \tag{14}$$

where

(i) $\beta(s) = \dfrac{1}{1 + s}$

(ii) $\ln \beta(s) = \lambda \left\{ 1 - \left(1 + \dfrac{2s}{\lambda} \right)^{1/2} \right\}$

$1/\lambda$ being the variance of the inverse normal distribution which we have chosen to be $\frac{1}{2}$. We used seven different methods of evaluating the corresponding formula (10) and one procedure of a different kind. The results are shown in Table 3.3.

We first observe that there is an explicit formula for $f(x, t)$ when $p_n(t)$ is Poisson and $b(\cdot)$ is exponential with unit mean. We derived this following (2.15) and can write it as

$$f(x, t) = te^{-t-x} \sum_{n=1}^\infty \frac{(tx)^{n-1}}{n!(n-1)!}$$

$$= e^{-t-x} \sqrt{t/x} \cdot I_1(2\sqrt{tx}) \tag{15}$$

Table 3.3.

	Number of sub-intervals $t = x$	Exponential			$t = x$	Inverse normal		
		10	100	1000		10	100	1000
Exact	–	0.08751	0.02816	0.00892		–	–	–
Trapezoidal	128	0.09104	0.02816	0.00892		0.10179	0.03254	0.01030
	256	8752	2816	892		10179	3254	1030
	512	8751	2816	892		10179	3254	1030
	1024	8751	2816	892		10179	3254	1030
Filon	512	0.08467	0.02816	0.00892		0.10179	0.03254	0.01030
	1024	8731	2816	892		10179	3254	1030
Tuck	1024	0.08479	0.02815	0.00891		0.10171	0.03253	0.01029
Clendenin	512	0.07706	0.02815	0.00889		0.10147	0.03252	0.01025
	1024	8479	2815	891		10171	3253	1029
Einarsson	1024	0.08750	0.02816	0.00892		0.10179	0.03254	0.01030
Squire's Generalized Midpoint	1024	0.08886	0.02816	0.00892		0.10183	0.03254	0.01031
Vooren and Linde	–	0.08737 (100)	0.02814 (6)	0.00892 (16)		0.10166 (16)	0.03252 (7)	0.01030 (20)
Stehfest	$N = 16$	0.08728	0.00033	neg.		0.10106	0.02187	0.00254
	$N = 18$	8743	27	neg.		10150	2362	284
	$N = 20$	8750	14	5×10^{-6}		10166	2516	313

For $y = 2\sqrt{tx} \geqslant 3.75$ Olver (1964, Section 9.8.4) has provided an eighth degree polynomial in $3.75/y$ for $I_1(y)$ which is in error by less than 2.2×10^{-7}. We used this to obtain the three 'exact' five decimal values at the head of Table 3.3.

Mathematically the simplest method of quadrature of the integral in (10) is the use of the trapezoidal rule repeated suitably often over the u-range $(0, T)$. In fact an iterative time-saving procedure was used on the computer – the program is provided in connection with GETUWT of the Appendix – so that an initial single trapezium of base $(0, T)$ was split into two trapezia of bases $(0, T/2)$ and $(T/2, T)$, respectively. Each of these trapezia was split into two and so on. The whole range $(0, T)$ was thus covered successively by 1, 2, 4, ... 1024 trapezia and in each case the aggregate area of the trapezia whose ordinates are those of the integrand of (10) was evaluated. The results, provided in Table 3.3, are excellent even after using as few (in computer terms) as 256 trapezia. Even more importantly it appears that, once T has been chosen appropriately, the successive doubling of the number of trapezia provides a valid indication of the convergence of the aggregate area to the true value (Seal, 1977b). We mention that we have used (10) rather than the simpler (11); the choice between these formulas is somewhat difficult as has been illustrated numerically in Seal (1977b).

The general trapezoidal approximation to the first term of (10) is

$$\frac{e^{cx}h}{\pi}\left\{ \sum_{j=0}^{N} P(jh)\cos(jhx) - \tfrac{1}{2}P(0) - \tfrac{1}{2}P(Nh)\cos(Nhx) \right\} \tag{16}$$

where $P(\cdot)$ is the real component of $\gamma(\cdot)$ and $Nh = T$. It thus remains to explain how c and T were chosen.

By the Central Limit theorem the distribution of the sum of n identical random variables tends to the Normal as $n \to \infty$. Relation (1.8) thus indicates that $f(x, t)$ tends to normality as t, which controls the number of terms in the sum that are not essentially zero, increases without bound. The distribution of $X(t)$ is thus bell-shaped and its mode is near its mean $E\{X(t)\} = t$. This is why we have chosen $x = t$ in Table 3.3.

A notable feature of Table 3.3 is the wide range of $t-$, and thus of $x-$, values. If the numerical value of (10) is to be of the order of 10^{-1} or 10^{-2} for x ranging between 10 and 1000 it is clear that c in the factor e^{cx} must be quite small, say about 10^{-2} or 10^{-3}, if this factor is not to dominate the calculations. Our conclusion has been to choose $c = 0$ although we recognize that there is possibly some non-zero value which optimizes the quadrature (Dubner and Abate, 1968). Such trials with different c-values were not appropriate for Table 3.3.

In order to select T-values which produced small values of the integrand of (10) a series of preliminary trials suggested the following six values. The corresponding values of $P(\cdot)$ and $Q(\cdot)$, which may oscillate in a damped manner, indicate the size of the leading term in (12).

	Exponential $t = x$ 10	100	1000	Inverse normal $t = x$ 10	100	1000
T	20π	$\tfrac{1}{3}$	$\tfrac{1}{10}$	10	$\tfrac{2}{5}$	$\tfrac{1}{8}$
$P(T)$	-4×10^{-7}	7×10^{-6}	2×10^{-6}	-2×10^{-5}	10^{-5}	-10^{-6}
$Q(T)$	-7×10^{-6}	4×10^{-5}	5×10^{-5}	2×10^{-5}	10^{-5}	10^{-5}

The trapezoidal method of quadrature takes no account of the nature of the integrands of $C(x)$ and $S(x)$ which oscillate rapidly even when T is as small as shown. In Filon's method (Davis and Rabinowitz, 1975, Section 2.10.2; FORTRAN program in their Appendix 2) the interval $(0, T)$ is divided into an even number of subintervals over each successive pair of which $P(u)$, or $Q(u)$, is approximated by a parabola 'fitted' at the mid and two end ordinates. This permits the 'exact' treatment of the oscillating cosine (or sine) factor and would appear to be a promising substitute for the simple trapezoidal. Table 3.3, however, shows that when t is fairly small the procedure may be inferior to the trapezoidal.

A simplified Filon uses straight lines for $P(\cdot)$, or $Q(\cdot)$, over each subinterval and produces a trapezoidal formula with a 'factor' multiplying each term (Davis and Rabinowitz, 1975, Section 2.10.2). When the range of integration is infinite the method reduces to multiplication of the whole (repeated) trapezoidal formula by

$$\left(\frac{\sin\left(\frac{hx}{2}\right)}{\frac{hx}{2}}\right)^2$$

(Tuck, 1967). Although our T-values are sometimes quite small increasing them to infinity would not change the trapezoidal results. We may therefore utilize the above multiplier with the unsatisfactory results shown in Table 3.3.

A Filon-type formula has been proposed by Clendenin (1966) for Fourier integrals with infinite range (Davis and Rabinowitz, 1975, Section 3.9). It is, perhaps, interesting to note that Tuck's (1967) underestimates in Table 3.3 were reproduced by those of the more complicated Clendenin formulas.

Another Filon-type procedure reported by Davis *et al.* was that of Einarsson (1972) with its associated FORTRAN procedure. Although $\cos(ux)$ completes 100 periods (each of 2π) in the exponential case with $x = 10$ none of these Filon-based formulas turns out to be as good as the simple Trapezoidal.

The foregoing formulas denominated as of Filon-type were all based on low degree polynomial approximations to $P(\cdot)$, or $Q(\cdot)$, over each panel or pair of panels. Vooren and Linde (1966) on the other hand give formulas that are exact if $P(\cdot)$ is of seventh degree and if $Q(\cdot)$ is of the eighth over each panel. From our viewpoint the novelty is that p, the number of panels in each of which $P(\cdot)$ or $Q(\cdot)$ is evaluated at 16 points, is given by $Tx = 2\pi p$ and thus depends on x. We have shown the appropriate p-values in Table 3.3 in parentheses. Although all the results are reasonably close to the truth, and sometimes depend on relatively few calculations, the method does not provide an approximation for all occasions.

We used one other quadrature method that appears in Squire (1970). It is well-known, and indeed obvious, that the repeated trapezoidal rule can be replaced by a rule in which the mean of the ordinates at the ends of the base of each trapezium is replaced by the ordinate at the midpoint of this base. Squire (1970, Section 5.5) has applied the linear Filon property to the repeated midpoint rule and has supplemented each function value with a correction involving its derivative. Table 3.3 does not find this procedure particularly attractive.

All the foregoing inversions of (14) are based on quadrature of (9) or (10). There are, however, a large number of formulas based directly on the relation immediately preceding (9) (Krylov and Skoblya, 1969) some of which were discussed in Seal (1969, Appendix B). Among these are the, at first sight, promising expansions using Laguerre polynomials (Seal, 1969) but Seal (1975) has shown how unsatisfactory these have been in risk theoretic applications. We could only find a single article in Neuts's (1976) bibliography that appeared to use numerical inversion of Laplace transforms to produce functions of interest in queueing theory. This was the Nance *et al.* (1972) article in which three different methods of inversion were tried on the Laplace–Stieltjes transform of the distribution function of the length of the busy period in a time-sharing system. One of these methods was the use of relation (11) with a variable c (mentioned above) and another was the Laguerre expansion already referred to. The third method was that of Stehfest (1970) and was chosen as the preferred technique which 'produced values substantially the same' as relation (11) without its 'slight oscillatory behavior'.

Consider the probability density

$$f_n(z) = na\binom{2n}{n}(1 - e^{-az})^n e^{-naz} \qquad 0 < z < \infty \tag{17}$$

which has its mode at $z = \ln 2/a$ and a variance that tends to zero as n increases. We then have

$$C_n \equiv \int_0^\infty g(z)f_n(z)dz = na\binom{2n}{n}\sum_{i=0}^n \binom{n}{i}(-1)^i\gamma(\overline{n + i} \cdot a)$$

$$\sim g\left(\frac{\ln 2}{a}\right) \qquad \text{for } n \text{ large}$$

This formula requires the use of $(n + 1)$ values of $\gamma(s)$ and with $a = \ln2/x$ an approximation for $g(x)$ is obtained. However Stehfest (1970) proposes to use a linear combination of C_n ($n = 1, 2, \ldots N/2$) with N even by means of the following Abel identity (Riordan, 1968, p. 18, and his Table 1.2)

$$A_{N/2-1}(-N/2, 1; 0, -j) \equiv \sum_{i=0}^{N/2-1} \binom{N/2-1}{i}(-N/2 + i)^{i+0}(1 + \overline{N/2-1} - i)^{N/2-1-i-j}$$

$$= \sum_{i=0}^{N/2-1} \binom{N/2-1}{i}(-1)^i (N/2 - i)^{N/2-1-j}$$

$$= A_{N/2-1}(1, -N/2; -j, 0)$$

$$= \left.\begin{matrix} 0 \\ 1 \end{matrix}\right\} \quad \begin{matrix} j = 1, 2, 3, \ldots \\ j = 0 \end{matrix} \tag{18}$$

Introducing the 'constant' C_n

$$g(x)A_{N/2-1}(-N/2, 1; 0, -j) \sim \sum_{i=1}^{N/2} \binom{N/2-1}{i-1}(-1)^{i-1}(N/2 + 1 - i)^{N/2-1-j}C_{N/2+1-i}$$

$$= \frac{\ln 2}{x} \sum_{i=1}^{N/2} \frac{(-1)^{i-1}(N/2 + 1 - i)^{N/2-1}}{(N/2 - i)!(i - 1)!} \frac{(N + 2 - 2i)!}{(N/2 + 1 - i)!(N/2 - i)!}$$

$$\times \sum_{j=0}^{N/2+1-i} \binom{N/2 + 1 - i}{j}(-1)^j\gamma\left(\overline{N/2 + 1 - i + j} \cdot \frac{\ln 2}{x}\right)$$

$$= \frac{\ln 2}{x} \sum_{k=1}^{N/2} \frac{(-1)^{N/2-k}k^{N/2-1}}{(k - 1)!(N/2 - k)!} \frac{(2k)!}{k!(k - 1)!} \sum_{j=0}^k \binom{k}{j}(-1)^j\gamma\left(\overline{k+j} \cdot \frac{\ln 2}{x}\right)$$

$$= \frac{\ln 2}{x} \sum_{k=1}^{N/2} \frac{(-1)^{N/2-k}k^{N/2-1}(2k)!}{(N/2 - k)!(k - 1)!(k - 1)!k!} \gamma\left(k\frac{\ln 2}{x}\right)$$

$$+ \frac{\ln 2}{x} \sum_{j=1}^{N/2}\sum_{k=j}^{N/2} \frac{(-1)^{N/2-k}k^{N/2-1}(2k)!(-1)^j}{(N/2 - k)!(k - 1)!(k - 1)!j!(k - j)!} \gamma\left(\overline{k+j} \cdot \frac{\ln 2}{x}\right) \tag{19}$$

This was the formula we used with N in the neighbourhood of 18 which Stehfest found was about the optimum on a computer working in 16-digit arithmetic (as the CDC 6500 does). Nevertheless, as we have indicated, a number of alternative values was tried for N. Contrary to the queueing theory experience this procedure produces poor results.

* * * * * * * * *

The surprising conclusion of our numerical experiments is the choice of a simple trapezoidal formula for the inversion of Laplace transforms occurring in risk theory.

REAL AND IMAGINARY FORMS OF $\beta(s)$

It remains to identify the forms of $\beta(s)$ that have been used in risk theory and to provide their analysis by the formula

$$\beta(s) = \beta(c + iu) = R(u) + iI(u)$$

It has been mentioned in Chapter 2 that the two most popular choices for $b(\cdot)$ are the Pareto and the lognormal distributions. Neither of these has a Laplace transform $\beta(s)$ so the foregoing inversion methods to obtain $f(x, t)$ are not immediately applicable. Instead we must evaluate an approximation to $\beta(s)$ by means of the formula

$$R(u) + iI(u) = \beta(s) \simeq \sum_{n=0}^{N} e^{-sn}b(n) = \sum_{n=0}^{N} e^{-cn}\{\cos(un) - i\sin(un)\}b(n)$$

with appropriately small steps in the n-values and N chosen so that $b(N)$ is very small (say 10^{-5}), and calculate

$$p_n(t)\{\beta(s)\}^n = p_n(t)\{A(u) + iB(u)\}$$

with

$$A(u) = \{R^2(u) + I^2(u)\}^{n/2} \cos\left\{n \arctan \frac{I(u)}{R(u)}\right\}$$

and

$$B(u) = \{R^2(u) + I^2(u)\}^{n/2} \sin\left\{n \arctan \frac{I(u)}{R(u)}\right\}$$

for $n = 0, 1, 2, \ldots$ (or for $n = 0, \Delta, 2\Delta, \ldots$ with a view to using Lubbock's formula), subsequently summing the results and inverting by means of (10). However to use (10) the foregoing calculations must be made for a large number of values of $s = c + iu$, c being constant, and it needs no emphasis that a mathematical form for $\beta(s)$ and suitable choice of $p_n(t)$ is far preferable from a computational viewpoint. Some of the possibilities were indicated in Chapter 2.

The Laplace transforms of the exponential and inverse normal distributions with unit means were given earlier in this chapter. With means equal to μ their analyses into real and imaginary parts are as follows:

(i) $\quad \beta(s) = \dfrac{1}{s + 1/\mu} = \dfrac{1}{c + 1/\mu + iu} = \dfrac{c + 1/\mu - iu}{(c + 1/\mu)^2 + u^2}$

so that

$$R(u) = \frac{c + 1/\mu}{(c + 1/\mu)^2 + u^2} \quad \text{and} \quad I(u) = \frac{-u}{(c + 1/\mu)^2 + \mu^2} \tag{20}$$

(ii) $\quad \beta(s) = \exp\left[\dfrac{\lambda}{\mu}\left\{1 - \left(1 + \dfrac{2\mu^2 s}{\lambda}\right)^{1/2}\right\}\right]$

Write

$$\left(1 + \frac{2\mu^2 s}{\lambda}\right)^{1/2} = A e^{iB}$$

then

$$1 + \frac{2\mu^2(c + iu)}{\lambda} = A^2 e^{2iB} = A^2 \cos(2B) + iA^2 \sin(2B)$$

Equating real and imaginary parts

$$1 + \frac{2\mu^2}{\lambda} c = A^2 \cos(2B)$$

$$\frac{2\mu^2 u}{\lambda} = A^2 \sin(2B)$$

i.e.

$$\frac{\dfrac{2\mu^2 u}{\lambda}}{1 + \dfrac{2\mu^2 c}{\lambda}} = \tan(2B)$$

and

$$\left(1 + \frac{2\mu^2 c}{\lambda}\right)^2 + \left(\frac{2\mu^2 u}{\lambda}\right)^2 = A^4$$

whence A and B in terms of λ, μ, c and u. Finally

$$\beta(s) = \exp\left[\frac{\lambda}{\mu}(1 - Ae^{iB})\right]$$

$$= e^{\lambda/\mu} \exp\left[-\frac{\lambda A}{\mu} \cos B - i\frac{\lambda A}{\mu} \sin B\right]$$

$$= e^{(\lambda/\mu) - (\lambda A/\mu)\cos B}\left\{\cos\left(\frac{\lambda A}{\mu} \sin B\right) - i \sin\left(\frac{\lambda A}{\mu} \sin B\right)\right\} \tag{21}$$

It is sometimes convenient to write $\beta(s)$ as

$$R(u) + iI(u) \equiv T(u)e^{iS(u)}$$
$$\equiv T(u)\cos\{S(u)\} + iT(u)\sin\{S(u)\}$$

so that

$$R(u) = T(u)\cos\{S(u)\}$$

and

$$I(u) = T(u)\sin\{S(u)\}$$

implying

$$\frac{I(u)}{R(u)} = \tan\{S(u)\} \tag{22}$$

and

$$R^2(u) + I^2(u) = T^2(u) \tag{23}$$

CHAPTER 4

The Probability of t-year Survival

We are now ready to calculate the probability of a non life insurance company surviving (at least) t time intervals. We have already written $U(w, t)$ for this probability given that the company has a risk (or 'free') reserve of w at the beginning of the interval $(0, t)$ and assuming (implicitly) that the risk loading on the pure unit level annual premium, payable continuously throughout the year — a very important requirement — is $100\eta\%$. Expenses of administration which are usually forecast and loaded into the premium are ignored; that is to say they are assumed to occur exactly as envisioned.

AN OPERATIONAL FORMULA FOR $U(w, t)$

Like Reich (1961), who solved a very similar problem, we will utilize a number of indicator random variables: $X_{\mathcal{U}}$ is defined as the indicator random variable of the set $\mathcal{U}$ where

$$X_{\mathcal{U}} = \begin{cases} 1 & \text{if } x_{\mathcal{U}} \text{ is a member of } \mathcal{U} \\ 0 & \text{if } x_{\mathcal{U}} \text{ is not a member of } \mathcal{U}, \text{ i.e., is a member of not-} \mathcal{U} \end{cases}$$

Hence

$$E\{X_{\mathcal{U}}\} = 1 \times \Pr\{X_{\mathcal{U}} \in \mathcal{U}\} + 0 \times \Pr\{X_{\mathcal{U}} \in \text{not-}\mathcal{U}\}$$
$$= \Pr\{X_{\mathcal{U}} \in \mathcal{U}\}$$

Let us consider the random variable

$$D(\tau) = \pi_1 \tau - X(\tau), \qquad X(0) = 0, \qquad 0 \leqslant \tau \leqslant t$$

where $X(\tau)$ represents the aggregate claims that have occurred in the interval $(0, \tau)$ and $\pi_1 \tau$ (with $\pi_1 = 1 + \eta$) is the aggregate premium paid during that interval. If the risk reserve at $\tau = 0$ is w the probability we are seeking is that $D(\tau)$ does not sink below $-w$ (i.e., the risk reserve, $w + D(\tau)$, does not become negative) during the interval $(0, t)$. The stochastic process $D(\cdot)$ with decremental amounts equal to the claims that occur is supposed to continue through $\tau = t$ whether or not ruin has occurred.

Write $X_{S_w(a,b)}$ for the indicator random variable of the set of realizations of $D(\cdot)$ in which $D(\tau)$ does not sink below $-w$ during the interval (a, b). Thus, e.g.

$$X_{S_w(0,t)} = \begin{cases} 1 & \text{if there is no ruin in } (0, t) \\ 0 & \text{otherwise} \end{cases}$$

and write $X_{C(\tau)}$ for the following indicator random variable

$$X_{C(\tau)} = \begin{cases} 1 & \text{if } D(\tau) \geqslant -w \\ 0 & \text{if } D(\tau) < -w \end{cases}$$

Let us now construct an indicator random variable $X_{/\!/}$ for the set of realizations of $D(\cdot)$ which have ended the interval $(0, t)$ with $D(t) \geqslant -w$, namely in a state of non-ruin. Such realizations *either* never dropped below the line $-w$ so that $X_{S_w(0,t)} = 1$ *or* dropped below the line $-w$ once or more times but finally crossed back above it before epoch t at which point $D(t) \geqslant -w$. If we define $dX_{C(\tau)}$ to be the change in $X_{C(\tau)}$ from 0 to 1 as $D(\tau)$, on an upward path, reaches or crosses the line $-w$ at the epoch τ, the second alternative above can be written

$$\int_0^t X_{S_0(\tau, t)} dX_{C(\tau)}$$

the first factor in the integrand being 0 or 1 depending on whether there is or is not an epoch of ruin in the final interval (τ, t). Hence we may write

$$X_{/\!/} = X_{S_w(0,t)} + \int_0^t X_{S_0(\tau, t)} dX_{C(\tau)} = \begin{cases} 1 & D(t) \geqslant -w \\ 0 & D(t) < -w \end{cases}$$

Observing that

$$E\{X_{S_w(0,t)}\} = U(w, t) \qquad E\{X_{S_0(\tau, t)}\} = U(0, t - \tau)$$

$$E\{X_{C(\tau)}\} = \Pr\{D(\tau) \geqslant -w\} = \Pr\{\pi_1\tau - X(\tau) \geqslant -w\}$$

$$= \Pr\{X(\tau) \leqslant w + \pi_1\tau\} = F(w + \pi_1\tau, \tau)$$

$$E\{X_{S_0(\tau, t)} dX_{C(\tau)}\} = E\{dX_{C(\tau)}\} E\{X_{S_0(\tau, t)} \mid dX_{C(\tau)} = 1\}$$
$$= U(0, t - \tau) d_\tau F(w + \pi_1\tau, \tau)$$

and

$$E\{X_{/\!/}\} = E\{X_{C(t)}\} = F(w + \pi_1 t, t),$$

the expectation of $X_{/\!/}$ where $X_{/\!/}$ has been derived above is

$$F(w + \pi_1 t, t) = U(w, t) + \int_0^t U(0, t - \tau) d_\tau F(w + \pi_1\tau, \tau)$$

and thus

$$U(w, t) = F(w + \overline{1 + \eta} \cdot t, t) - (1 + \eta) \int_0^t U(0, t - \tau) f(w + \overline{1 + \eta} \cdot \tau, \tau) d\tau \quad (1)$$

The integrand on the right hand side of (1) may be interpreted as the product of two probabilities: (i) that at epoch τ the *past* aggregate claims exactly equal the initial reserve plus premiums paid, and (ii) given that the risk reserve is zero at epoch τ the *future* development of $D(\cdot)$ through epoch t will be free of ruin. Notice that the argument has been effected in terms of a continuous density for $X(\tau)$; an arbitrary w could not be added to the premiums received in the interval $(0, \tau)$ to produce a payable total of discrete claims.

Before proceeding it is desirable to review the assumptions made, either implicitly or explicitly, in establishing (1). We may list them as:

(i) In order that relation (1.10) should apply to any interval of length t without specific reference to its epoch of commencement $p_n(t)$ must likewise apply to any interval of length t on the relevant time scale.

(ii) Y, the random variable expressing the monetary amount of an individual claim, is independent of $N(t)$, the random variable expressing the number of claims occurring in $(0, t)$ – and, in fact, occurring in any interval of length t.

(iii) The n values of Y implied in $p_n(t)$ are realizations of independent random variables

The fundamental relation (1) was derived by Arfwedson (1950) in the special case $B(x) = 1 - e^{-x}$ but the general formulation first appeared in a dam problem in a paper by Gani and Prabhu (1959). Although the number of epochs at which water was supplied, corresponding to our number of claims, was specifically Poisson the article envisioned generalization to a certain type of mixed Poisson input and the development is to be found in Prabhu's textbook (1965, Chapter 7). In two 1960 articles which he later expanded into a monograph Beneš (1963) introduced the idea of a completely general input process for a queueing system, and produced (1) for the distribution function of the time a customer must wait for service if he arrives at epoch t, except that the $f(\cdot)$ in the integrand of (1) had to be replaced by a conditional probability that took into account that there was no queue at epoch τ. In risk theory this condition is empty provided $p_n(t)$ in (1.8) is a stationary point process, and (1) was accordingly extended by Seal (1969, 1974) to recognize this more general form of $p_n(t)$. In his 1961 article Prabhu had already pointed out that both (1) and (6) (below) applied when $p_n(t)$ is mixed Poisson with infinitely divisible mixing distribution (though differently expressed). This historical review is important because some queueing theoreticians have assured the author that (1) only applies for Poisson input.

Observe that (1) holds when $w = 0$ at which point $U(w, t)$ has a discontinuity. In general the resulting integral equation will have to be solved for $U(0, t)$. Nevertheless if $p_n(t)$ can be expressed as a simple or mixed Poisson process with infinitely divisible mixing distribution or as a so-called stuttering Poisson process there is an explicit formula for $U(0, t)$ which substantially simplifies the calculation of $U(w, t)$.

In deriving this formula we follow Prabhu (1965, Chapter 7, Section 7.5). We base our arguments on the model

$$Z(t) = u + X(t) - t$$

so that $Z(t)$ can be regarded as the aggregate claims through time t increased by a quantity u (which we will eventually replace by zero) and reduced by a 'premium' payable at a unit rate. In Prabhu's case $X(t)$ was the aggregate input of water into a dam which was being depleted at a uniform rate. We ask for the time $T(u)$ during which $Z(t) \geq 0$. Prabhu is correspondingly asking for the 'wet period' of the dam.

If the system runs for an interval $(0, u)$ Z is necessarily non-negative throughout and at the end of it we, as it were, start T again with the quantity u replaced by the aggregate claims (water input) at epoch u. Hence

$$T(u) = u + T[X(u)] \tag{2}$$

Writing

$$G(u, t) = \Pr\{T(u) \leq t\}$$

$$G(u, t) = \Pr\{T[X(u)] \leq t - u\} \qquad \text{from (2)}$$

$$= \int_0^{t-u} f(x, u)G(x, t - u)dx$$

We wish to solve this integral equation for $G(u, t)$.

Now the characteristic function of $X(t)$ or, equivalently, the Laplace-Stieltjes transform of $F(x, t)$ (t fixed) assumes a very special form when $p_n(t)$, the density function of $N(t)$, is of a certain type. In fact Thyrion (1969) proves that the necessary and sufficient condition for the relation

$$\int_{0-}^{\infty} e^{-sx} dF(x, t) = e^{-t\{1-\zeta(s)\}} \equiv e^{-t\xi(s)}$$

where the minus sign in the lower limit of the integral indicates that the integration is started just before $x = 0$ with $F(x, t) = 0$, and where $\zeta(s)$ is a Laplace transform which may involve t, is that the Laplace transform of $N(t)$ can be written in the form $e^{-t\{1-\nu(s)\}}$, $\nu(s)$ being the Laplace transform of a positive integer valued random variable. Thyrion (1969) shows that (i) certain mixed (compound) Poisson distributions of $N(t)$, and (ii) distributions of multiple events such that a Poisson event at epoch t produces a cluster of L claims where L is a random variable (stuttering Poisson processes), satisfy the foregoing criterion. In a further contribution Thyrion (1971/2) shows that the particular type of mixed Poisson has an infinitely divisible mixing distribution (Kendall and Stuart, 1977, Section 4.33). [Thyrion's theorems are expressed in terms of characteristic functions but there should be no difficulty in understanding our 'translation'.]

Assuming $p_n(t)$ to be of this special form consider

$$\frac{d}{ds} e^{-(t+r)\xi(s)} = (t + r)e^{-(t+r)\xi(s)}\{-\xi'(s)\}$$

$$= \frac{t + r}{t} e^{-r\xi(s)} \frac{d}{ds} e^{-t\xi(s)} \tag{3}$$

Now

$$\frac{d}{ds}e^{-t\xi(s)} = \frac{d}{ds}\left\{\int_0^\infty e^{-sx}f(x, t)dx + F(0, t)\right\} = -\int_0^\infty e^{-sx}xf(x, t)dx$$

and the product of two Laplace transforms is the Laplace transform of the convolution of the two functions involved. Hence (3) is equivalent to

$$\frac{t}{t+r}\int_0^\infty e^{-sx}xf(x, t+r)dx = \int_0^\infty e^{-sx}dx\int_0^x f(x-y, r)yf(y, t)dy$$

the term $F(0, r)$ at $y = x$ making no contribution to the integral, or

$$\int_0^\infty e^{-sx}dx\left[\frac{tx}{t+r}f(x, t+r) - \int_0^x f(x-y, r)yf(y, t)dy\right] \qquad \text{for all } s > 0$$

There results Prabhu's identity

$$\int_0^x yf(y, t)f(x-y, r)dy = \frac{tx}{t+r}f(x, t+r) \tag{4}$$

We will now prove that a solution of the integral equation for $G(u, t)$ is

$$G(u, t) = \begin{cases} 0 & t \leqslant u \\ \int_u^t \frac{u}{\tau}f(\tau - u, \tau)d\tau & t > u \end{cases} \tag{5}$$

For we have

$$\int_0^{t-u} f(x, u)G(x, t-u)dx = \int_0^{t-u} f(x, u)dx\int_x^{t-u} \frac{x}{\tau}f(\tau - x, \tau)d\tau \quad \text{by hypothesis}$$

$$= \int_0^{t-u} \frac{d\tau}{\tau}\int_0^\tau xf(x, u)f(\tau - x, \tau)dx$$

$$= \int_0^{t-u} \frac{u\tau}{u+\tau}f(\tau, u+\tau)\frac{d\tau}{\tau} \quad \text{by (4)}$$

$$= \int_u^t \frac{u}{y}f(y-u, y)dy$$

$$= G(u, t)$$

Note that, from (5), the density function of $T(u)$ is

$$\frac{\partial}{\partial t}G(u, t) = \frac{u}{t}f(t-u, t)$$

It remains to relate this argument based on $Z(t)$ to our own $R(t)$ in the special case where $R(0) = 0$. Prabhu's (1961) procedure is relevant here.

With a zero initial reserve survival through epoch t occurs if $R(t) = u \geqslant 0$ and

$R(\tau)$ has never been negative, $\tau < t$. Following the course of $R(\tau)$ *backwards* from $\tau = t$ we see that $R(t - \tau) = Z(\tau)$ of the foregoing development. Summing the density of $T(u)$ for all values of u

$$U(0, t) = \int_0^\infty \frac{u}{t} f(t - u, t)du = \frac{1}{t} \int_0^{t+} uf(t - u, t)du \quad \pi_1 = 1$$

$$= \frac{1}{t} \int_0^t F(t - u, t)du \quad \text{by 'parts'}$$

i.e.,

$$U(0, t) = \frac{1}{\pi_1 t} \int_0^{\pi_1 t} F(y, t)dy \quad \pi_1 \geqslant 1 \tag{6}$$

ARFWEDSON AND THYRION: AN IMAGINARY COLLABORATION

We have already mentioned that Prabhu (1961) introduced relations (1) and (6) to the actuarial profession – which completely ignored them! It is interesting to note, however, that the content of Prabhu's article was already implicit in the actuarial literature.

In his paper Prabhu first proved (1) and (6) for the Poisson/exponential case and then generalized these relations for any input $p_n(t)$ such that

$$\int_{0-}^\infty e^{-sx} dF(x, t) = e^{-t\xi(s)}$$

These results seem far removed from the actuarial formulae of the 1950's but observe that:

(a) In Arfwedson (1950) referring to Poisson/exponential formula (44) is, in different notation, (1) above;

(b) Arfwedson's (48) can be written

$$U(w, t) = F(w + \overline{1 + \eta} \cdot t, t) - (1 + \eta) \int_0^t e^{(t-z)\eta} f(w + \overline{1 + \eta} \cdot t, z)dz$$

so that

$$U(0, t) = F(\overline{1 + \eta} \cdot t, t) - (1 + \eta) \int_0^t e^{(t-z)\eta} f(\overline{1 + \eta} \cdot t, z)dz$$

$$= F(\overline{1 + \eta} \cdot t, t) - (1 + \eta) \int_0^t zf(\overline{1 + \eta} \cdot z, t)dz \quad \text{using a}$$
$$\text{procedure similar to that}$$
$$\text{developed following (2.15)}$$

$$= \int_0^{(1+\eta)t} \left(1 - \frac{z}{(1 + \eta)t}\right) f(z, t)dz$$

$$= \frac{1}{(1 + \eta)t} \int_0^{(1+\eta)t} F(z, t)dz \quad \text{by 'parts'}$$

and this is relation (6) above;

(c) Having thus set the scene with (1) and (6) for the Poisson/exponential case we notice that Thyrion (1959) proved that the df, $F(x, t)$, of a process $X(t)$ with Poisson claim occurrences could be identified with the $F(x, t)$ of a process $X(t)$ with claim occurrences given by

$$p_n(t) = \sum_{m=0}^{\infty} e^{-\lambda t} \frac{(\lambda t)^m}{m!} Q_n^{m*}$$

where Q_n is a discrete probability density, together with an appropriately adjusted $B(\cdot)$ dependent on t. The characteristic function of $X(t)$ is then

$$\exp\left[\lambda t \left\{ \sum_{n=0}^{\infty} Q_n \varphi^n(z) - 1 \right\}\right]$$

and is of the Prabhu form cited above. We may now extend (1) and (6), which depend only on $F(x, t)$ and its derivative $F(x, t)$, from the Poisson/exponential to any $X(t)$ with input $p_n(t)$ of the above general form.

NUMERICAL EVALUATION OF RELATION (1)

Once f, F and $U(0, \tau)$ of (1) have been calculated for values of τ progressing at chosen steps from zero through t the integral on the right-hand side may be computed by approximate integration. We have chosen 'repeated Simpson' for this purpose in subroutine REPSIM of program GETUWT of the Appendix supplementing it by the (Simpson's) three-eighths rule when there is an odd number of panels.

The calculation of $f(\cdot, t)$ and $F(\cdot, t)$ may be effected simultaneously for fixed w and η by inverting $s\psi_t(s)$ and $\psi_t(s)$, respectively, a formula for the former being derived in Chapter 3 just prior to (3.14). The function $U(0, t)$ responds to a similar treatment when (6) obtains, namely when $p_n(t)$ is mixed Poisson with infinitely divisible mixing distribution or stuttering Poisson, for then

$$U(0, t) = \frac{1}{(1 + \eta)t} \int_0^{(1+\eta)t} F(y, t) dy \qquad \text{by (6)}$$

$$= \frac{1}{(1 + \eta)t} \int_0^{(1+\eta)t} dy \frac{1}{2\pi i} \int_{c-i\infty}^{c+i\infty} e^{sy} \psi_t(s) ds$$

by (3.8) and the following relation

$$= \frac{1}{2\pi i} \int_{c-i\infty}^{c+i\infty} \psi_t(s) ds \frac{1}{(1 + \eta)t} \frac{e^{sy}}{s} \Bigg|_{s=0}^{(1+\eta)t}$$

$$= \frac{1}{2\pi i} \int_{c-i\infty}^{c+i\infty} \frac{\psi_t(s)}{(1 + \eta)t} \frac{e^{s(1+\eta)t}}{s} \{1 - e^{-s(1+\eta)t}\} ds \qquad (7)$$

By comparison with the relation preceding (3.9) this means that $U(0, t)$ is the inverse of the Laplace transform

$$\frac{1 - e^{-s(1+\eta)t}}{s(1 + \eta)t} \, \psi_t(s)$$

at the point $x = (1 + \eta)t$.

The results of Chapter 3 suggest that the individual functions involved in (1) are calculated correctly to five decimal places when 1024 or more terms are used in trapezoidal quadrature. Nevertheless this degree of accuracy with integral τ-values used in repeated Simpson only produces a bare four decimal accuracy in $U(w, t)$ (Seal, 1974, Tables 2 and 3).

When (6) is no longer available, as for instance is the case when generalized Waring is used for $p_n(t)$, $U(0, \tau)$ must be obtained by solution of the integral equation (1) with $w = 0$. We have included a subroutine INTEQN (developed in Chapter 5) in GETUWT that uses the repeated Simpson quadrature for the integral in (1) and we recommend that finer intervals than unity are used for τ in this part of the program even though this substantially increases the computer time required.

In Chapter 3 we proposed that trapezoidal quadrature be used to evaluate the integral in (3.10) and discussed how to choose an upper limit T to the integral. With some inefficiency a single value of T may be made to apply at every τ-value to all three of the transforms used when (6) applies. There is, however, one novelty: two of the transforms are infinite (have poles) when $s = c + iu = iu$ is zero. What we propose to do in these two cases (cp. Seal, 1977b) is to deform the Laplace transform $\gamma(s)$, say, by subtracting $1/s$ and subsequently use

$$\lim_{s \to 0} \left\{ \gamma(s) - \frac{1}{s} \right\}$$

as the zero term of the trapezoidal quadrature. Since the inverse of the Laplace transform $1/s$ is unity this must be added to the final inverse to adjust the deformation. This procedure would require the inversion of the Laplace transform $\gamma(s) - 1/s$ instead of $\gamma(s)$. As an alternative we may note that trapezoidal quadrature applied to the relation preceding (3.10) with $c = 0$ and $\gamma(c + iu) = 1/iu$ is (ignoring the zero term which has already been taken care of)

$$\frac{h}{2\pi} \sum_{j=1}^{\infty} \left\{ e^{ijhx} \frac{1}{ijh} - e^{-ijhx} \frac{1}{ijh} \right\} = \frac{hx}{\pi} \sum_{j=1}^{\infty} \frac{\sin(jhx)}{jhx}$$

$$= \frac{1}{2\pi} (\pi - hx) \tag{8}$$

We may thus use the trapezoidal quadrature on $\gamma(s)$ which has a pole of the form $1/s$ at $s = 0$ provided

    (i) the zero term is replaced by $\lim_{s \to 0} \left\{ \gamma(s) - \dfrac{1}{s} \right\}$, and

(ii) the final result is increased by

$$1 - \frac{1}{2\pi}(\pi - hx) = \frac{1}{2} + \frac{hx}{2\pi}$$

Let us therefore calculate the zero trapezoidal term for $\psi_t(s)$ and $\{1 - e^{s(1+\eta)t}\}\psi_t(s)/\{s(1 + \eta)t\}$. We have

$$\psi_t(s) - \frac{1}{s} = \frac{\sum\limits_{n=0}^{\infty} p_n(t)\{\beta(s)\}^n - 1}{s}$$

and since this is of the form 0/0 when $s \to 0$ we may use the rule of Hôpital to get

$$\sum_{n=1}^{\infty} np_n(t)\{\beta(s)\}^{n-1}\beta'(s) \to \beta'(0) \sum_{n=1}^{\infty} np_n(t) = \beta'(0)E\{N(t)\} = -t \qquad (9)$$

The form 0/0 is also assumed in the limit by

$$\frac{\{1 - e^{-s(1+\eta)t}\} \sum\limits_{n=0}^{\infty} p_n(t)\{\beta(s)\}^n - s(1 + \eta)t}{s^2(1 + \eta)t}$$

and on differentiating numerator and denominator separately we have

$$\frac{\{1 - e^{-s(1+\eta)t}\}\sum np_n(t)\{\beta(s)\}^{n-1}\beta'(s) + (1 + \eta)te^{-s(1+\eta)t}\sum p_n(t)\{\beta(s)\}^n - (1 + \eta)t}{2s(1 + \eta)t}$$

This fraction also takes the form 0/0 at $s \to 0$ so we get

$$\frac{1}{2(1 + \eta)t}(\{1 - e^{-s(1+\eta)t}\}\sum np_n(t)[\{\beta(s)\}^{n-1}\beta''(s) + (n - 1)\{\beta(s)\}^{n-2}\{\beta'(s)\}^2]$$

$$+ 2(1 + \eta)te^{-s(1+\eta)t}\sum np_n(t)\{\beta(s)\}^{n-1}\beta'(s)$$

$$- (1 + \eta)^2 t^2 e^{-s(1+\eta)t}\sum p_n(t)\{\beta(s)\}^n)$$

$$\to \frac{1}{2(1 + \eta)t}\left[-2(1 + \eta)t \sum_{n=1}^{\infty} np_n(t) - (1 + \eta)^2 t^2 \sum_{n=0}^{\infty} p_n(t)\right] = -t - \frac{1}{2}(1 + \eta)t$$

$$(10)$$

Seal's (1971) inversions of $\psi_t(s)$ for $t = 10$, 100 and 1000 by trapezoidal quadrature based on (3.10) showed that the most inaccurate results occurred when $t = 10$; in fact the accuracy gets worse as t decreases to unity. The Gaussian quadratures of Seal (1974), however, showed a surprising accuracy for the Poisson/exponential case even when $t = 1$ (Table 2, Seal, 1971). We have thus modified the 1974 computer program and include it in the Appendix as GETBRM for those who desire greater accuracy at the small (say, first half dozen) t-values

Table 4.1. Values of $U(0, t)$ and $U(10, t)$ with $\eta = 0.1$

$p_n(t)$	$B(y)$	Program	$t = 1$	2	3	4	5
Poisson	Exponential	UWT	0.53582	0.40699	0.34475	0.30668	0.28040
		BRM	0.53659	0.40713	0.34478	0.30669	0.28040
		UWT	0.9996	0.9987	0.9967	0.9940	0.9907
		BRM	0.9997	0.9986	0.9967	0.9941	0.9907
	Inverse Normal	UWT	0.47562	0.35739	0.30280	0.26982	0.24720
		BRM	0.47640	0.35753	0.30283	0.26983	0.24720
		UWT	0.9999	0.9998	0.9993	0.9985	0.9974
		BRM	1.	1.	0.9994	0.9984	0.9972
Negative binomial $h = 2$	Exponential	UWT	0.57998	0.47648	0.42982	0.40310	0.38573
		BRM	0.58091	0.47673	0.42992	0.40315	0.38576
		UWT	0.9989	0.9937	0.9826	0.9674	0.9495
		BRM	0.9989	0.9936	0.9826	0.9674	0.9495
	Inverse Normal	UWT	0.53092	0.43900	0.40050	0.37907	0.36538
		BRM	0.53186	0.43926	0.40060	0.37913	0.36542
		UWT	0.9996	0.9968	0.9885	0.9754	0.9590
		BRM	0.9999	0.9970	0.9885	0.9751	0.9583
Generalized Waring $a = 2, b = 4,$ $c = 8$	Exponential	INT(step 1/2)	1.	0.7067	0.5071	0.3717	0.2722
		INT(step 1/4)	1.	0.6801	0.4688	0.3130	0.1971
		UWT	1.	1.	1.	0.9856	0.9610
	Inverse Normal	INT(step 1/4)	1.	0.6103	0.4029	0.2614	0.1553
		UWT	1.	1.	1.	0.9924	0.9722

provided $p_n(t)$ is mixed Poisson with infinitely divisible mixing distribution or stuttering Poisson.

A sample of values of $U(0, t)$ and $U(10, t)$ produced by GETUWT and GETBRM is given in Table 4.1 for $t = 1, 2, \ldots 5$. The values of $U(0, t)$ when $p_n(t)$ is generalized Waring have been calculated by the integral equation (1) and a comparison of the values at steps of $\frac{1}{2}$ and $\frac{1}{4}$ suggest that it would be presumptuous to say that four-decimal accuracy has been achieved by the latter. The most surprising conclusion from the Table is that within this range of t-values and for all three choices for $p_n(t)$ $U(10, t)$, the probability of survival, increases when one moves from the exponential for $b(\cdot)$ to the more 'dangerous', i.e., longer tailed, Inverse Normal.

BEARD'S FORMULA FOR $W_n(w)$

Towards the end of Chapter 2 we mentioned Beard's (1971) suggestion that the epoch through which survival of an insurance enterprise was measured could be the epoch of occurrence of the nth claim rather than the time required for t expected claims. The probability of this alternative survival was written $W_n(w)$ when the initial risk reserve is w and results from queueing theory indicated that intervals between claims had to be independent, namely form a renewal process, for this probability to be calculable. Although renewal processes other than the Poisson process are a field for theoreticians rather than practical men let us generalize Beard's (1971) formula in a form explicitly given by Lindley (1952) and implicit in much of the earlier work of Pollaczek.

Write

$G(x) =$ Pr {amount subtracted from risk reserve at the first claim or
        between occurrence of two claims $\leqslant x$} $-\infty < x < \infty$

      $=$ Sum over y of Pr{a claim is of size $\leqslant x + \pi_1 \nu$ when one occurs
        after an inter-claim interval of length y}

$$= \int_{\max(0,\,-x/\pi_1)}^{\infty} B(x + \pi_1 y)dA(y) \qquad (11)$$

It follows that

$$W_{n+1}(w) = \int_{-\infty}^{w} W_n(w - x)dG(x) \qquad n = 0, 1, 2, \ldots \qquad (12)$$

with

$$W_0(w) = 1 \quad w \geqslant 0$$

In general these formulas will have to be evaluated by approximate integration and we have used the simple Poisson/exponential case to exemplify the technique in a computer program entitled POLLAK in the Appendix. This is based on

$$g_+(x) \equiv \int_0^{\infty} b(x + \pi_1 y)a(y)dy = e^{-x} \int_0^{\infty} e^{-(1+\pi_1)y}dy = \frac{e^{-x}}{1 + \pi_1} \quad x > 0 \quad (13)$$

$$g_-(x) \equiv \int_{-x/\pi_1}^{\infty} b(x + \pi_1 y)a(y)dy = \frac{e^{x/\pi_1}}{1 + \pi_1} \quad x < 0 \quad \pi_1 = 1 + \eta = 1.1 \quad (14)$$

In the more general case these two functions (FCT and FCTNEG in the program) may have to be evaluated by approximate integration for each x-value. This would materially increase the computing time which was 15 seconds for the program exhibited. Only the first four integer values of n were evaluated for w proceeding in steps of one-tenth from 0.1 to 10 (100 values). Comparison with Table 2.6 indicates that errors are of the order of one to three units in the fifth decimal place. Further experiments are desirable if extensive use were to be made of this program.

CHAPTER 5

Approximations and Controls

Table 3.3 showed that the quadratures involved in the numerical inversions of Laplace transforms occasionally produce results far from the correct values. For this reason it is useful to have available:

(1) approximate methods of calculation of $f(x, t)$, $F(x, t)$ and $U(w, t)$ which do not utilize Laplace transforms; and

(2) independent methods of calculating $U(w, t)$ for values of t increasing without bound, namely $U(w)$.

It is the purpose of this chapter to provide such methods.

APPROXIMATIONS TO $F(x, t)$

The 1963/4 paper by Bohman and Esscher was basically concerned with the approximate numerical calculation of $F(x, t)$ in the cases where $p_n(t)$ was Poisson or negative binomial. The Esscher method developed some 30 years earlier proved the most accurate but the much simpler incomplete gamma function ratio had 'an astonishing accuracy in large parts of the field investigated'. The latter was restricted to $x \geq t$, $t \geq 100$ and to negative binomial indices $h \geq 20$. The first restriction does not disturb us since the first argument of F and f in (4.1) is always at least equal to the value of the second. Small t and h values were used in Seal (1971) and required more detailed calculations, and small t-values necessarily inhibit the use of methods developed for large t.

A few years after the Bohman–Esscher paper Kauppi and Ojantakanen (1969) proposed to treat the variate y given by the quadratic

$$y + \frac{\kappa_3/\kappa_2^{3/2}}{3!} (y^2 - 1) = \frac{x - t}{\sqrt{\kappa_2}}$$

where the kappas are the cumulants of the distribution function F, as a $N(0, 1)$ variable and thus approximate F by Φ, the Normal distribution function. The suggestion was well received by workers in this area and it was not until Seal (1977a) that it was realized that the results were generally not as accurate as those of the Bohman–Esscher gamma formula.

The latter is written

$$F(t + z\sqrt{\kappa_2}, t) \simeq \frac{1}{\Gamma(\alpha)} \int_0^{\alpha + z\sqrt{\alpha}} e^{-y} y^{\alpha - 1} dy \equiv P(\alpha, \alpha + z\sqrt{\alpha}) \qquad (1)$$

in standard incomplete gamma function ratio notation, where

$$\alpha = \frac{4\kappa_2^3}{\kappa_3^2} \quad \text{a function of } t,$$

and $P(\cdot)$ may be read from Khamis's (1965) tables remembering that his second argument has to be doubled to conform with our notation. Table 4 in Seal's 1977 article compares the two methods in a variety of cases. Table 5.1, taken from Seal (1978), shows in the first two of its three comparisons the gamma approximation

Table 5.1. *Values of f(10 + t, t), F(10 + t, t) and U(10, t)*

t	$f(10 + t, t)$		$F(10 + t, t)$		$U(10, t)$	
	Following (2)	Exact	(1)	Exact	(1) and (2)	Method of 1974 paper
1	0.00004	0.00003	0.99996	0.99997	0.9999	1.0000
2	0.00019	0.00016	0.99978	0.99983	0.9997	1.0000
3	0.00049	0.00045	0.99937	0.99945	0.9991	0.9993
4	0.00095	0.00090	0.99866	0.99879	0.9980	0.9981
5	0.00154	0.00150	0.99764	0.99779	0.9964	0.9964
6	0.00226	0.00222	0.9963	0.9965	0.9943	0.9943
7	0.00305	0.00303	0.9947	0.9948	0.9916	0.9915
8	0.00390	0.00390	0.9927	0.9929	0.9884	0.9883
9	0.00479	0.00479	0.9906	0.9908	0.9847	0.9846
10	0.00569	0.00570	0.9882	0.9884	0.9807	0.9804
11	0.00658	0.00661	0.9857	0.9858	0.9762	0.9759
12	0.00747	0.00750	0.9830	0.9831	0.9715	0.9711
13	0.00833	0.00837	0.9801	0.9803	0.9665	0.9660
14	0.00916	0.00921	0.9772	0.9774	0.9613	0.9607
15	0.00997	0.01002	0.9742	0.9744	0.9559	0.9552
16	0.01074	0.01079	0.9711	0.9713	0.9503	0.9495
17	0.01147	0.01153	0.9680	0.9682	0.9447	0.9438
18	0.01217	0.01223	0.9649	0.9651	0.9369	0.9380
19	0.01283	0.01289	0.9618	0.9619	0.9331	0.9321
20	0.01346	0.01352	0.9586	0.9588	0.9273	0.9262
21	0.01406	0.01411	0.9554	0.9556	0.9214	0.9202
22	0.01462	0.01467	0.9523	0.9524	0.9155	0.9143
23	0.01515	0.01520	0.9491	0.9493	0.9097	0.9083
24	0.01564	0.01570	0.9460	0.9462	0.9038	0.9024
25	0.01611	0.01617	0.9429	0.9431	0.8980	0.8965

and the exact value, respectively, of the f and F functions. Here $p_n(t)$ is Poisson with mean t and the density function of individual claim sizes is inverse Gaussian, namely

$$b(x) = \left(\frac{\lambda}{2\pi x^3} \right)^{1/2} \exp\left[-\frac{\lambda(x - \mu)^2}{2\mu^2 x} \right] \quad 0 < x < \infty$$

with $\mu = 1$ and $\lambda = 2.20408$. We see that even when t is small the gamma approximation is quite good and we recommend that it be used as a control whenever values of f or F are being calculated by numerical inversion of their Laplace transforms.

APPROXIMATE CALCULATION OF $U(w, t)$

As far as we know there have only been four approximations proposed for $U(w, t)$. Seal's (1969a, with FORTRAN program) Monte Carlo simulation procedure calculates the value of $U(w, t)$ by tracking by computer N risk businesses each of which starts with a given value of w and suffers claims at random in accordance with a selected random process T which is simulated on the computer by pseudo-random numbers. Whenever a claim occurs it is the realization of a simulated random variable Y. The business is followed until its reserve plus loaded premium intake is exhausted (ruin) or until it survives the chosen period t (non-ruin). A count of the cases of ruin among the N businesses provides the proportion ruined in the period $(0, t)$. Seal's (1969a) article describes the computer time required for different choices of T and Y and it is obvious that this is proportionate to the value of t chosen. [Seal's choice of $N = 60,000$ was based on the fallacious general argument that the number of businesses ruined is a binomial random variable. The premium rate for companies designated $XI/\cdot/1$ was, by error, not held constant at $1 + \eta$.]

The first approximation to $U(w, t)$ by mathematical methods was Beekman and Bowers's (1972) formula for the Poisson/general case in which the first two moments of the random variable

$$Z_t = \max_{0 \leqslant \tau \leqslant t} \{X(\tau) - \tau(1 + \eta)\}$$

and a formula for $\Pr\{Z_t = 0\}$ were used to derive an expression for $1 - U(w, t)$ that involved the incomplete gamma ratio. The extensive numerical examples provided by these authors show that the method cannot be relied upon to produce even one-decimal accuracy. For example, $U(10, 10)$ with $\eta = 0.1$ is 0.97 when $B(\cdot)$ is a triple mixed exponential which roughly graduates the Swedish fire insurance data of Cramér (1955, p. 43), in comparison with a true value of 0.86. A similar comment applies to the indications offered by Beard (1975) who proposed to approximate the two terms of (4.1), the first by the Bohman—Esscher gamma, namely (1) above, and the second by a Pearson Type I or Type III curve. Beard only gives meager numerical results and they do not look very promising.

The writer's own (1978) development of the Bohman–Esscher gamma approximation for f and F is based on relation (4.6) for $U(0, t)$, namely

$$
U(0, t) = \frac{1}{(1 + \eta)t} \int_0^{(1+\eta)t} F(y, t)\,dy
$$

$$
= \frac{\sqrt{\kappa_2}}{(1 + \eta)t} \int_{-t/\sqrt{\kappa_2}}^{\eta t/\sqrt{\kappa_2}} F(t + z\sqrt{\kappa_2}, t)\,dz
$$

$$
\simeq \frac{\sqrt{\kappa_2}}{(1 + \eta)t} \int_{-t/\sqrt{\kappa_2}}^{\eta t/\sqrt{\kappa_2}} P(\alpha, \alpha + z\sqrt{\alpha})\,dz \quad \text{by (1)}
$$

$$
= \frac{\sqrt{(\kappa_2/\alpha)}}{(1 + \eta)t} \int_{\alpha - t\sqrt{(\alpha/\kappa_2)}}^{\alpha + \eta t\sqrt{(\alpha/\kappa_2)}} P(\alpha, u)\,du
$$

$$
= \frac{1}{(1 + \eta)t\beta} \int_{\alpha - t\beta}^{\alpha + \eta t\beta} \frac{du}{\Gamma(\alpha)} \int_0^u x^{\alpha - 1} e^{-x}\,dx \quad \text{with } \beta = \sqrt{(\alpha/\kappa_2)}
$$

$$
= \frac{1}{(1 + \eta)t\beta\Gamma(\alpha)} \left[\int_0^{\alpha + \eta t\beta} (\alpha + \eta t\beta - x) x^{\alpha - 1} e^{-x}\,dx \right.
$$

$$
\left. - \int_0^{\alpha - t\beta} (\alpha - t\beta - x) x^{\alpha - 1} e^{-x}\,dx \right]
$$

$$
= \frac{1}{(1 + \eta)t\beta} \left[(\alpha + \eta t\beta)P(\alpha, \alpha + \eta t\beta) - \alpha P(\alpha + 1, \alpha + \eta t\beta) \right.
$$

$$
- (\alpha - t\beta)P(\alpha, \alpha - t\beta) + \alpha P(\alpha + 1, \alpha - t\beta)] \tag{2}
$$

In order, therefore, to calculate $U(w, t)$ from (4.1) F is found from (1), f by differentiating that relation, namely

$$
f(t + z\sqrt{\kappa_2}, t) \simeq \frac{\beta}{\Gamma(\alpha)} e^{-\alpha - z\sqrt{\alpha}} (\alpha + z\sqrt{\alpha})^{\alpha - 1}
$$

and $U(0, \tau)$ is obtained from (2). In order to approximate the integral in (4.1) repeated Simpson may be used. The penultimate column of Table 5.1 was based on unit steps in t; when t was odd the last three panels were approximated by the three-eighths rule; the trapezoidal was used for $t = 1$. In this somewhat limited, but essentially practical, example the extension of the Bohman–Esscher gamma approximation is working very well and we suggest it be used whenever rough values of $U(w, t)$ are needed as controls of the quadratures of the prior chapter. As soon as t exceeds 10 an electronic computer is needed to perform the approximate integration and to avoid excessive reference to Khamis's (1965) tables.

It occurred to the writer that the De Moivre lemma of Chapter 3 could be used to obtain approximate values of $U(w, t)$ even when $b(\cdot)$ has no Laplace transform as in the lognormal or Pareto cases. The derivation of (4.1) required that $b(\cdot)$, and thus $f(\cdot, t)$, should be continuous but if the steps in the claim amounts underlying

b_j are relatively small the error in using (4.1) and (4.6) on the $f(x, t)$ and $F(x, t)$ produced by DEMOIV at the beginning of Chapter 3 should not be great.

As an example let us try to reproduce some of the values of Table 2.5 (i.e., with $\eta = 0$) assuming that we can write

$$B(j) = 1 - e^{-\mu j} \qquad j = 0, 1, 2, \ldots$$

so that

$$b(j) = B(j) - B(j - 1) \quad j = 1, 2, 3, \ldots$$
$$= e^{-\mu(j-1)} - e^{-\mu j}$$

and

$$b(0) + \sum_{j=1}^{\infty} b(j) = b(0) + 1 = 1 \quad \text{with } b(0) = 0.$$

The mean of this distribution is

$$\sum_{j=1}^{\infty} jb(j) = - \sum_{j=1}^{\infty} j\Delta e^{-\mu(j-1)}$$

$$= -\left[je^{-\mu(j-1)} \Big|_{1}^{\infty} + \sum_{j=1}^{\infty} e^{-\mu j} \right] \text{ by 'parts' (Steffensen, 1927, Section 102)}$$

$$= \frac{1}{1 - e^{-\mu}}$$

Choosing $\mu = 0.2231435513$ this mean equals 5. The mean of the assumed Poisson input was taken as $t/5$ so the premium rate is unity.

De Moivre's lemma is then used to produce $f(x, t)$ and $F(x, t)$ for $t = 1, 2, 3, \ldots$ (which correspond in our case to $\frac{1}{5}, \frac{2}{5}, \frac{3}{5}, \ldots$ 'years') and

$$U(0, t) \simeq \frac{1}{t} \sum_{j=0}^{t} F(j, t) - \frac{1}{2t} \{p_0(t) + F(t, t)\}$$

Then with w in the unit chosen for $b(\cdot)$ we have

$$U(w, t) = F(w + t, t) - \int_{0}^{t} U(0, t - \tau)f(w + \tau, \tau)d\tau$$

The integral has to be approximated with t and τ given integer values and repeated Simpson is convenient for this purpose.

The program DEMUWT of the Appendix produced the following values which are compared with those of Table 2.5. The computing time required, namely 17 seconds, is on the high side but the procedure is promising in view of its generality and the avoidance of Laplace transforms.

	$j = 1$	2	3	4	5
$U(0, 5j)$	0.531	0.391	0.321	0.278	0.248
Table 2.5	0.524	0.386	0.319	0.278	0.249
$U(50, 5j)$	1.000	0.999	0.998	0.995	0.992
Table 2.5	1.000	0.999	0.996	0.993	0.989

CALCULATION OF $U(w)$

It remains to discuss methods of calculating $U(w)$, the probability of eternal survival of a nonlife insurance company. If $p_n(t)$ is Poisson this becomes a very well-worked field.

Referring to Cramér (1955, equation 85) or to Seal (1969, 4.43) we see that for the Poisson/general case where $U(0) = \eta/(1 + \eta)$

$$U(w) = \frac{\eta}{1 + \eta} + \int_0^w U(w - y) \frac{1 - B(y)}{1 + \eta} \, dy \tag{3}$$

This integral equation could be solved numerically by one of the methods described (with rather lengthy FORTRAN computer programs) in Atkinson (1976) but we wondered if a naive application of repeated Simpson (with the three-eighths rule at one end when w is odd) might not be satisfactory. In fact this technique has already been used in GETUWT when $p_n(t)$ is generalized Waring. Thus, choosing h suitably small, and starting with the trapezoidal

$$U(h) \simeq \frac{\eta}{1 + \eta} + \frac{h}{2} \left[U(h)k(0) + U(0)k(h) \right]$$

where

$$k(y) = \frac{1 - B(y)}{1 + \eta} \quad \text{and} \quad U(0) = \frac{\eta}{1 + \eta} = \eta k(0)$$

so that

$$U(h) \simeq \left\{ 1 - \frac{h}{2(1 + \eta)} \right\}^{-1} \frac{\eta}{1 + \eta} \left[1 + \frac{h}{2} k(h) \right]$$

Simpson once applied produces

$$U(2h) \simeq \left\{ 1 - \frac{h}{3(1 + \eta)} \right\}^{-1} \left[\frac{\eta}{1 + \eta} + \frac{h}{3} \left\{ 4U(h)k(h) + \frac{\eta}{1 + \eta} k(2h) \right\} \right]$$

It is easy to see what changes are called for with repeated Simpson. The use of the three-eighths rule may be illustrated on $U(7h)$:

$$U(7h) = \frac{\dfrac{h}{3}}{1 - \dfrac{h}{3(1 + \eta)}} \left\{ \frac{3\eta}{h(1 + \eta)} + 4k(h)U(6h) + 2k(2h)U(5h) + 4k(3h)U(4h) \right.$$

$$\left. + k(4h)U(3h) + \frac{9}{8} \left[k(7h)U(0) + 3k(6h)U(h) + 3k(5h)U(2h) + k(4h)U(3h) \right] \right\}$$

The FORTRAN program UINTEG of the Appendix illustrates the use of this procedure in the Poisson/exponential case with $\eta = 0.1$. As can be seen we chose $h = 0.1$ and wrote $[1 - B(\cdot)]/(1 + \eta)$ as $HH(\cdot)$. The computer produced 400 values of $U(w)$, as well as the corresponding true values (Seal, 1969, p. 121)

$$U(w) = 1 - \frac{1}{1 + \eta} \exp\left[-\frac{\eta w}{1 + \eta} \right]$$

in nine seconds of calculation time. All results except the first (based on the trapezoidal) were correct to five decimal places. At first sight this is rather promising because $U(40) = 0.97605$ and a relatively small addition to the uppermost value of w should produce 'near certainty' in the probability of indefinite survival. Unfortunately, as we shall see, this satisfactory result was not repeated for more practical choices of $b(\cdot)$.

What might be termed the classic approximation for $U(w)$ in the Poisson/general case is that of F. Lundberg (Seal, 1969, p. 131), namely

$$1 - U(w) \sim \frac{\eta}{-\beta'(-\kappa) - 1 - \eta} e^{-\kappa w} \tag{4}$$

where $\beta(\cdot)$ is the Laplace—Stieltjes transform of $B(\cdot)$ and κ is the smallest positive root of the equation

$$\beta(-\kappa) = 1 + \kappa(1 + \eta)$$

Other approximations have been proposed for the Poisson/general case. That of Beekman—Bowers (Beekman, 1969) makes use of the incomplete gamma ratio. It is

$$U(w) \simeq \frac{\eta}{1 + \eta} + \frac{1}{1 + \eta} \int_0^w \frac{x^{\alpha - 1} e^{-x/\beta}}{\Gamma(\alpha)\beta^\alpha} \, dx = \frac{\eta}{1 + \eta} + \frac{1}{1 + \eta} P(\alpha, w/\beta) \tag{5}$$

where

$$\beta = \frac{2}{3} \frac{E(Y^3)}{E(Y^2)} + \frac{E(Y^2)}{2\eta} (1 - \eta)$$

and

$$\alpha = \frac{E(Y^2)}{2\eta\beta}(1 + \eta)$$

and avoids the awkward root-solving of the Lundberg formula.

It has been suggested by Ryder (1976, Appendix,III) that in the Poisson/general case the moments of Y up to the fifth could be used with the Cornish–Fisher transformation to Normality (Kendall and Stuart, 1977, p. 175) based on the Cramér Laplace transform of $U(\cdot)$ (Seal, 1969, p. 120). Unfortunately the author only gives a single three-decimal numerical example for the Poisson/exponential case with $\eta = 0.1$ and $w = 10$.

Grandell and Segerdahl (1971) made a series of comparisons of the Lundberg and Beekman–Bowers methods of approximation with

$$B'(y) = \frac{a^a}{\Gamma(a)} y^{a-1} e^{-ay} \quad 0 < y < \infty; a > 0$$

The 'exact' values were obtained from an explicit formula due to 0. Thorin. With $\eta = 0.1$ and a taking the values 10^{-k}, $k = 1, 2, 3$ – all J-shaped distributions – nine or ten large values of w for each k showed that the Lundberg approximation was never worse, and sometimes better, than the simpler Beekman–Bowers value. On the other hand, on the last page of Beekman (1969) a comparison of the two approximations based on Cramér's (1955, p. 43)

$$B'(y) = 4.897954e^{-5.514588y} + 4.503(y + 6)^{-2.75} \quad 0 < y < 500$$
$$= 0 \quad y > 500$$

a graduated version of Swedish non-industrial fire insurance claims in 1948–51, and five values of w showed a clear superiority for the Beekman–Bowers formula.

In order to test the Beekman–Bowers approximation on further examples we first tried it on the Grandell–Segerdahl (1971) gamma distribution with $a = \frac{1}{10}$ but for small values of w. The supposedly exact value was the Simpson approximation of (3) with suitably small h-value. As before 400 values of $U(w)$ were calculated for equidistant multiples of h. Table 5.2 shows the disappointing results. It would seem that four-decimal accuracy is barely achieved for the repeated Simpson approximation to (3) when $h = 0.01$; the third decimal may be two or three units in error when $h = 0.1$. The Beekman–Bowers approximation has errors of up to four units in the third decimal place for $w < 1$ but the error seems to be increasing as w approaches unity. Further experiments were deemed unnecessary since the gamma distribution has never been fitted successfully to actual claims data, so far as the writer knows.

The second set of trials was on the popular lognormal distribution for $b(\cdot)$. Using the seventh of Ferrara's (1971) nine distributions the second and third moments about zero with unit mean were

$$p_2 = 97.001 \quad \text{and} \quad p_3 = 912{,}692$$

Table 5.2 shows that there seems to be some slight improvement in the integral equation solutions with $h = 0.1$: results appear to be correct to the third decimal place. However, the Beekman–Bowers formula is apparently approximating a different function. Perhaps a hint of the reason is Johnson and Kotz's (1970) statement that the moments of the lognormal can belong to a different distribution. Until these peculiar results have been explained we are reluctant to recommend the use of the Beekman–Bowers approximation to $U(w)$.

All the foregoing methods are based on $U(w)$ directly or on its moments. However the Laplace transform of $U(w)$ is (Cramér, 1930, p. 79, or Seal, 1969, p. 120)

$$\frac{\eta}{(1 + \eta)s - 1 + \beta(s)}$$

and this can sometimes be put into a form that is easily inverted. For example when $B(\cdot)$ is exponential and $\beta(s) = (1 + s)^{-1}$ the foregoing Laplace transform analyses into linear partial fractions and an explicit form emerges for $U(w)$ (Seal, 1969, pp. 120–121). Similar remarks hold when $B(\cdot)$ has a gamma form with integral index so that $\beta(s) = (s + a)^{-a}$ (a an integer).

When T is other than exponential, and thus $p_n(t)$ other than Poisson, we are much more restricted. Ammeter (1948) extended the Lundberg approximation to the negative-binomial/general case (implying that successive T-values are not

Table 5.2. Values of U(w)

	Gamma					Lognormal		
	(3) with $h =$			0.1	(5)	(3) with $h =$		(5)
w	0.001	0.005	0.01	0.1		0.001	0.1	
0.01	0.0913	0.0914	0.0915	–	0.0911	0.0917	–	0.4168
0.02	0.0917	0.0918	0.0918	–	0.0913	0.0924	–	0.4352
0.03	0.0921	0.0921	0.0922	–	0.0915	0.0930	–	0.4465
0.04	0.0924	0.0925	0.0929	–	0.0917	0.0936	–	0.4548
0.1	0.0943	0.0943	0.0944	0.0967	0.0929	0.0966	0.0974	0.4823
0.2	0.0970	0.0971	0.0971	0.0987	0.0947	0.1006	0.1009	0.5044
0.3	0.0995	0.0996	0.0996	0.1015	0.0965	0.1038	0.1043	0.5180
0.4	0.1019	0.1019	0.1020	0.1037	0.0983	0.1067	0.1071	0.5279
1.0	–	0.1144	0.1145	0.1166	0.1085	–	0.1204	0.5609
3.0	–	–	–	0.1521	0.1403	–	0.1479	0.6038
6.0	–	–	–	0.1983	0.1844	–	0.1753	0.6329
10.0	–	–	–	0.2539	0.2385	–	0.2028	0.6553

independent) but we are not aware of any investigation into its accuracy. On the other hand the Cramér equation (3) becomes

$$U(w) = \int_{-\infty}^{0} U(w - z)g_-(z)dz + \int_{0}^{w} U(w - z)g_+(z)dz$$

where

$$g_+(z) = (1 + \eta) \int_{0}^{\infty} b(z + \overline{1 + \eta} \cdot y)dA(y)$$

$$g_-(z) = (1 + \eta) \int_{-z/(1+\eta)}^{\infty} b(z + \overline{1 + \eta} \cdot y)dA(y)$$

(cf. Seal, 1969, p. 121 with misprint in definition of $w(\tau)$ corrected) in the case where T-values are independent and thus form a renewal process. Unfortunately no observational examples of renewal processes occur in the risk theoretic or queueing literatures.

APPENDIX

Computer Programs

There follow eight FORTRAN programs that produced most of the numerical results of the preceding chapters. BESSEL is limited to the Poisson/exponential case and we do not expect it to be used very often. TRIALS has been included so that the reader can add other formulas to those included in Table 3.3. GETUWT and GETBRM produce the results for which this book was written. DEMOIV and DEMUWT obtain similar answers without using Laplace transforms. POLLAK is a rather expensive method of producing $W_n(w)$ and is subject to generalization. UINTEG is Cramér's integral equation solution of $U(w)$ for the Poisson/general case.

BESSEL

This program produces $U(w, t)$ for Poisson/exponential using (2.10) and (2.12). The incomplete gamma function ratio $P(k, w)$ is programmed as $P(K, IW)$ and all the needed values are obtained by means of the subroutine GAB. If K becomes too large the capacity of the computer will be exceeded. BES0 equalling I_0 of (2.11) is calculated and IBM's SSP subroutine BESI used for $BI(1) = I_1$ and $BI(2) = I_2$. The remaining modified Bessel functions through $BI(21) = I_{21}$ are found by recursion. This completes the calculation of the basic functions apart from their multiplication by convenient factors.

$Q 0 = q_0(10)$ and $Q(K) = q_k(10)$ are then found from (2.10) for k up to 20 and $U(w, 10)$ finally found from (2.12).

```
      PROGRAM BESSEL(INPUT,OUTPUT,TAPE5 =INPUT,TAPE6=OUTPUT)
      DIMENSION P(20,10),Q(20),BI(21),IER(2),U(10,10)
      WRITE(6,15)
   15 FORMAT(1H1)
      R=1.0/1.1
      S=SQRT(1.1)
      T=10.0
C     TWENTY TERMS OF MAIN SUM USED. LAST VALUE THUS Q(20)*P(20,IW)
      DO 1 IW=1,10
```

```
      GAM=1.0
      DO 2 K=1,20
      GAM=GAM*FLOAT(K)
      CALL GAB(FLOAT(K),FLOAT(IW)*1.0,G)
      P(K,IW)=G*FLOAT(K)/GAM
    2 CONTINUE
    1 CONTINUE
      WRITE(6,21)
      WRITE(6,6) (P(20,J),J=1,10)
C     21      BESSEL FUNCTIONS MULTIPLIED BY EXP(-2.0*T*S)
      DO 3 K=1,2
      CALL BESI(2.0*T*S,K,BIK,IERK)
      BI(K) = BIK
      IER(K) = IERK
    3 CONTINUE
      WRITE(6,6) IER
      DO 7 K=3,21
      BI(K) = BI(K-2) - 2.0*FLOAT(K-1)*BI(K-1)/(2.*T*S)
    7 CONTINUE
      DO 12 K=1,21
      BI(K)=EXP(-2.0*T*S)*BI(K)
   12 CONTINUE
      WRITE(6,19)
      WRITE(6,20)
      WRITE(6,6) BI
      X=2.0*T*S
      Z=(T*S)**2
      BES0=1.0+Z
      FAC=1.0
      Y=Z
      DO 9 J=2,50
      Y=Y*Z
      FAC=FAC*FLOAT(J)*FLOAT(J)
      BES0 = BES0 + Y/FAC
      IF(Y*EXP(-X)/FAC.LE.4.0E-08) GO TO 13
    9 CONTINUE
   13 BES0=BES0*EXP(-2.0*T*S)
      WRITE(6,19)
      WRITE(6,18)
      WRITE(6,6) BES0
    6 FORMAT(10E13.6)
C     Q IS P OF TAKACS. TWENTY TERMS OF BI  USED
      Q0=BES0+BI(1)/SQRT(R)
      D=SQRT(R)
      DO 10 K=2,20
      D=D*SQRT(R)
      Q0=Q0+(1.-R)*BI(K)/D
   10 CONTINUE
      Q0=Q0*EXP(-2.1*T)*EXP(2.0*T*S)
      WRITE(6,6) Q0
      WRITE(6,19)
      WRITE(6,17)
      DO 4 K=1,20
      C=R**(FLOAT(K)/2.0)
      Q(K)=C*BI(K)
      C=C/SQRT(R)
      Q(K) = Q(K) + C*BI(K+1)
      Q(K) = Q(K)*EXP(2.0*T*S)*EXP(-2.1*T)
      D=(1.-R)*R**K
      TERM0=1.0
      SUM0=1.0
      K1=K+1
      DO 16 M=1,K1
      TERM0=TERM0*1.1*T/FLOAT(M)
      SUM0=SUM0+TERM0
   16 CONTINUE
```

```
      TERM=1.0
      CONST=EXP(-2.1*T)
      SUM=CONST*SUM0
      DO 5 IR=1,30
      TERM=TERM*T/FLOAT(IR)
      TERMM=1.0
      SUMM=1.0
      M1=K+1+IR
      DO 14 M=1,M1
      TERMM=TERMM*1.1*T/FLOAT(M)
      SUMM=SUMM+TERMM
   14 CONTINUE
      SUM = SUM + TERM*SUMM*CONST
    5 CONTINUE
      V=TERM*SUMM*CONST*D
      WRITE(6,6) V
      Q(K) = Q(K) + D*(1.0-SUM)
    4 CONTINUE
      WRITE(6,19)
      WRITE(6,23)
      WRITE(6,6) Q
      DO 8 IW=1,10
      SUM=Q0
      DO 11 K=1,20
      SUM=SUM+Q(K)*P(K,IW)
   11 CONTINUE
      U(IW,10)=SUM
    8 CONTINUE
      WRITE(6,19)
      WRITE(6,22)
      WRITE(6,6) (U(IW,10),IW=1,10)
   17 FORMAT(2X,33HLAST TERM IN FINAL SUM FOR EACH K)
   18 FORMAT(2X,11HBES0 AND Q0)
   19 FORMAT(1H0)
   20 FORMAT(2X,31H21 BESSEL FUNCTIONS WITH FACTOR)
   21 FORMAT(2X,26HINCOMPLETE GAMMA FUNCTIONS)
   22 FORMAT(2X,14HU(W,10) VALUES)
   23 FORMAT(2X,29H20 QUEUE LENGTH PROBABILITIES)
      STOP
      END



      SUBROUTINE GAB(A,B,G)
C     FORMULA (11) OF KHAMIS(1965) MULTIPLIED BY GAMMA(A)
C     PRODUCES P(A,B) TO 7 DECIMALS WITH OCCASIONAL LAST PL. UNIT ERROR
      TERM = 1.0/A
      P=B**A*EXP(A)
      Q=A**A*EXP(B)
      SUM = TERM
      DO 1 K=1,50
      TERM = TERM*B/(A+FLOAT(K))
      IF(P*TERM/Q.LE.4.0E-08) GO TO 2
      SUM = SUM + TERM
    1 CONTINUE
    2 G = SUM*B**A*EXP(-B)
      RETURN
      END



      SUBROUTINE BESI(X,N,BI,IER)
C     REPRINTED BY PERMISSION FROM SYSTEM/360 SCIENTIFIC SUBROUTINE
C     PACKAGE VERSION III(1968) BY INTERNATIONAL BUSINESS MACHINES CORP.
      IER=0
      BI=1.0
      IF(N) 150,15,10
   10 IF(X) 160,20,20
   15 IF(X) 160,17,20
```

```
17 RETURN
20 TOL = 1.E-7
   IF(X-12.) 40,40,30
30 IF(X-FLOAT(N)) 40,40,110
40 XX=X/2.
50 TERM = 1.0
   IF(N) 70,70,55
55 DO 60 I=1,N
   FI = I
   IF(ABS(TERM)-1.E-68) 56,60,60
56 IER=3
   BI=0.0
   RETURN
60 TERM=TERM*XX/FI
70 BI=TERM
   XX=XX*XX
   DO 90 K=1,1000
   IF(ABS(TERM)-ABS(BI*TOL)) 100,100,80
80 FK=K*(N+K)
   TERM = TERM*(XX/FK)
90 BI = BI + TERM
100 RETURN
110 FN=4*N*N
   IF(X-170.0) 115,111,111
111 IER = 4
   RETURN
115 XX=1./(8.*X)
   TERM = 1.
   BI = 1.
   DO 130 K=1,30
   IF(ABS(TERM)-ABS(TOL*BI)) 140,140,120
120 FK=(2*K-1)**2
   TERM=TERM*XX*(FK-FN)/FLOAT(K)
130 BI=BI+TERM
   GO TO 40
140 PI=3.141592653
   BI=BI*EXP(X)/SQRT(2.*PI*X)
   GO TO 100
150 IER=1
   GO TO 100
160 IER=2
   GO TO 100
   END
```

DEMOIV

Discrete densities $f(x, t)$ and their cumulation $F(x, t)$ are calculated by means of De Moivre's lemma cited at the beginning of Chapter 3. As an illustration $p_n(t)$ is chosen as Poisson with $t = 20$ and the values of the claim densities b_j, $j = 1, 2, 3, \ldots m$ with $m = 79$ are lognormal areas. The suppression of the tails of the convolutions of b_j are effected to eight decimal places to achieve five figure accuracy in $F(x, t)$. Alternative input is complete when $P(\cdot)$ and $B(\cdot)$ have been programmed.

```
PROGRAM DEMOIV(INPUT,OUTPUT,TAPE5 =INPUT,TAPE6=OUTPUT)
DIMENSION B(79),X(80),Y(500),Z(500),BN(51)
DIMENSION P(50)
DIMENSION F(500),SF(500)
WRITE(6,1)
T=20.0
P0=EXP(-AMIN1(T,30.0))
```

```
C      CALCULATE POISSON WITH MEAN 20

       FAC=1.0
       DO 7 J=1,20
       FAC=FAC*FLOAT(J)
     7 CONTINUE
       P(20)=EXP(-T)*T**T/FAC
       DO 8 J=1,26
       P(J+20)=P(J+19)*T/FLOAT(20+J)
     8 CONTINUE
       DO 6 J=1,19
       J1=20-J
       P(J1)=P(J1+1)*FLOAT(21-J)/T
     6 CONTINUE

C      CALCULATE B(.) THE INDIVIDUAL CLAIM AMOUNT DISTRIBUTION

       NTOP=46
       B0=0.0
       IDIMX=80
       X(1)=B0
       DO 3 J=1,49
       XJ = 4000.0*FLOAT(J)
       A = 1.07353*ALOG10(XJ-70.0) - 2.433437
       CALL BIGPHI(A,PJ)
       BN(J) = PJ
     3 CONTINUE
       B(1) = BN(1)
       DO 4 J=2,49
       B(J) = BN(J) - BN(J-1)
     4 CONTINUE
       DO 9 J=50,78
       B(J)=0.0000200
     9 CONTINUE
       B(79)=0.0000016
       SUM=0.0
       DO 10 J=1,79
       SUM=SUM+B(J)
    10 CONTINUE
       WRITE(6,194)
       WRITE(6,5) B
       WRITE(6,204) SUM

C      CALCULATE CONVOLUTIONS OF B(.) THROUGH NTOP

       WRITE(6,2)
       DO 198 J=2,IDIMX
       X(J)=B(J-1)
       Y(J)=X(J)
   198 CONTINUE
       IDIMY=IDIMX
       ISTART=0

C      THE PRINT-OUT FOR ANY N IS THE NTH CONVOLUTION,N=2,3,...

       DO 199 N=1,NTOP
       IF(N.EQ.1) GO TO  206
       DO 200 JJ=1,IDIMZ
       IF(Z(JJ) .GT.4.0E-8) IFIRST=JJ
       IF(Z(JJ) .GT.4.0E-8)  GO TO 201
   200 CONTINUE
   201 DO 202 JK=1,IDIMZ
       JJJ=IDIMZ-JK+1
       IF(Z(JJJ).GT.4.0E-8) ILAST=JJJ
       IF(Z(JJJ).GT.4.0E-8) GO TO 203
   202 CONTINUE
   203 IDIMY=ILAST-IFIRST+1
       IFIR1=IFIRST-1
```

```
      ISTART=ISTART+IFIR1
      WRITE(6,197) N
      WRITE(6,196) ISTART
      WRITE(6,207) (Z(L),L=IFIRST,ILAST)
      WRITE(6,2)
C     CALCULATE SMLF(X,T) AND BIGF(X,T)

      IBOT=ISTART
      ITOP=ISTART+ILAST-IFIRST
      DO 211 IX=IBOT,ITOP
C     THE I-VALUES RUN FROM IFIRST TO ILAST

      I=IX-IBOT+IFIRST
      F(IX)=F(IX)+P(N)*Z(I)
  211 CONTINUE
      IF(N .EQ.NTOP) GO TO 199
      DO 205 JL=1,IDIMY
      JM=IFIRST+JL-1
      Y(JL)=Z(JM)
  205 CONTINUE
  206 CALL PMPY(Z,IDIMZ,X,IDIMX,Y,IDIMY)
  199 CONTINUE
      DO 210 IX=1,79
      F(IX)=F(IX)+P(1)*B(IX)
  210 CONTINUE
      SF(1)=F(1) + P0
      DO 212 IX=2,ITOP
      SF(IX)=SF(IX-1)+F(IX)
  212 CONTINUE
      WRITE(6,195)
      WRITE(6,207) (F(L),L=1,ITOP)
      WRITE(6,2)
      WRITE(6,207) P0
      WRITE(6,207) (SF(L),L=1,ITOP)
    1 FORMAT(1H1)
    2 FORMAT(1H0)
    5 FORMAT(1H ,10E13.5)
  194 FORMAT(2X,18HTHE DENSITIES B(.))
  195 FORMAT(2X,24HTHE ARRAYS SMLF AND BIGF)
  196 FORMAT(2X,25HSTARTING NUMBER OF CLAIMS  I4)
  197 FORMAT(2X,15HCONVOLUTION NO.  I4)
  204 FORMAT(2X,E15.8)
  207 FORMAT(2X,10E13.6)
  208 FORMAT(2X,I6)
      STOP
      END


      SUBROUTINE PMPY(Z,IDIMZ,X,IDIMX,Y,IDIMY)
C     REPRINTED BY PERMISSION FROM SYSTEM/360 SCIENTIFIC SUBROUTINE
C     PACKAGE VERSION III(1968) BY INTERNATIONAL BUSINESS MACHINES CORP.
      DIMENSION Z(1),X(IDIMX),Y(IDIMY)
      IF(IDIMX*IDIMY) 10,10,20
   10 IDIMZ=0
      GO TO 50
   20 IDIMZ=IDIMX+IDIMY-1
      DO 30 I=1,IDIMZ
   30 Z(I)=0.0
      DO 40 I=1,IDIMX
      DO 40 J=1,IDIMY
      K=I+J-1
   40 Z(K)=X(I)*Y(J)+Z(K)
   50 RETURN
      END
```

```
      SUBROUTINE BIGPHI(Y,F)
      AY=ABS(Y)
      T = 1.0/(1.0+.2316419*AY)
      F = 1.330274429
      F = F*T - 1.821255978
      F = F*T + 1.781477937
      F = F*T - .356563782
      F = F*T + .319381530
      F = F*T
      D=0.398942280*EXP(-Y*Y/2.0)
      F=F*D
      IF(Y) 1,2,2
    2 F=1.0-F
    1 RETURN
      END
```

TRIALS

This program provides seven methods of approximation of the Laplace transform inversion formula (3.10) and an inversion method due to Stehfest (1970) applied in the form (3.19). Details of its use were provided in Chapter 3 in connection with Table 3.3.

```
      PROGRAM TRIALS(INPUT,OUTPUT,TAPE5 =INPUT,TAPE6=OUTPUT)
C     TESTS OF VARIOUS QUADRATURE METHODS ON SMLF OF M/M/1
      DIMENSION FACT(24)
      DIMENSION PVTC(7),PVTS(7)
      EXTERNAL F,FF,AP
      DATA PI/3.14159265358980/
      WRITE(6,107)
  107 FORMAT(1H1)
      T=1000.0
      BIGT=1.0/10.0
      X=1000.0
      N=1024
      WRITE(6,7)
      WRITE(6,5) T,BIGT,X
    7 FORMAT(2X,18HVALUES OF T,BIGT,X)
      WRITE(6,6)

C     TRAPEZOIDAL

      CALL FTSTAR(0.0,T,RSMF,USMF)
      ZERORD=RSMF
      CALL FTSTAR(BIGT,T,RSMF,USMF)
      WRITE(6,101)
  101 FORMAT(2X,50HREAL AND IMAGINARY PARTS OF THE LT AT THE BOUNDARY)
      WRITE(6,5) RSMF,USMF
      WRITE(6,6)
    5 FORMAT(10E13.6)
      U=BIGT
      SUMMSF=(ZERORD+RSMF*COS(X*U)-USMF*SIN(X*U))*BIGT/2.0
      NN=1
    2 NN=2*NN
      NN1=NN/2
      H=BIGT/FLOAT(NN)
      SUMSF=0.0
      DO 1 I=1,NN1
      U=FLOAT(2*I - 1)*H
      CALL FTSTAR(U,T,RSMF,USMF)
      SUMSF=SUMSF+2.0*H*(RSMF*COS(X*U)-USMF*SIN(X*U))
```

```
   1 CONTINUE
     SUMMSF=(SUMMSF+SUMSF)/2.0
     SMLFF=SUMMSF/PI
     TK=SIN(H*X/2.0)/(H*X/2.0)
     TUCK=SMLFF*TK*TK
     WRITE(6,3) NN,SMLFF,TUCK
   3 FORMAT(I5,5X,2E13.6)
     IF(NN.EQ.N) GO TO 4
     GO TO 2
   4 WRITE(6,6)
   6 FORMAT(1H0)

C     FILON-DAVIS-RABINOWITZ-CLENDENIN

     WRITE(6,102)
 102 FORMAT(2X,19HFILON AND CLENDENIN)
     DO 16 J=1,3
     N=256*(J+MAX0(0,J-2))
     H=BIGT/FLOAT(N)
     TH=X*H
     A=0.0
     B=BIGT
     SUM=0.0
     CALL FTSTAR(0.0,T,RSMF,USMF)
     F1=RSMF
     FF1=USMF
     CALL FTSTAR(BIGT,T,RSMF,USMF)
     F2=RSMF
     FF2=USMF
     S1=SIN(A*X)
     S2=SIN(B*X)
     C1=COS(A*X)
     C2=COS(B*X)
     A1=A+H
     SR=F2*S2-F1*S1
     SR1=-.5*(F2*C2-F1*C1)
     SR2=SR1
     N1=N-1
     DO 19 I=1,N1,2
     CALL FTSTAR(A1,T,RSMF,USMF)
     SUM=SUM+RSMF*COS(A1*X)
     A1=A1+H
     CALL FTSTAR(A1,T,RSMF,USMF)
     SR1=SR1+RSMF*COS(A1*X)
     A1=A1+H
  19 CONTINUE
     CALL ALBEGA(TH,AL,BE,GA)
     FILON=H*(AL*SR+BE*SR1+GA*SUM)
     CLENDN=H*(SR1-SR2+SUM)
     SU=FF1*C1-FF2*C2
     SU1=-.5*(FF2*S2-FF1*S1)
     SU2=SU1
     A1=A+H
     SUM=0.0
     DO 18 I=1,N1,2
     CALL FTSTAR(A1,T,RSMF,USMF)
     SUM=SUM+USMF*SIN(A1*X)
     A1=A1+H
     CALL FTSTAR(A1,T,RSMF,USMF)
     SU1=SU1+USMF*SIN(A1*X)
     A1=A1+H
  18 CONTINUE
     FILON=(FILON-H*(AL*SU+BE*SU1+GA*SUM))/PI
     Z=2.0*SIN(X*H/2.)/(X*X*H)
     CLENDN=CLENDN-H*(SU1-SU2+SUM)
     CLENDN=CLENDN*4.0*SIN(X*H/2.)*SIN(X*H/2.)/(X*H*X*H)
```

```
      CLENON=CLENON+F1*Z*SIN(X*H/2.)+F2*(SIN(X*BIGT)/X-Z*SIN(X*(BIGT-
     1 H/2.)))-FF1*(1.0/X-Z*COS(X*H/2.))-FF2*(-COS(X*BIGT)/X+Z*COS(X*
     2 (BIGT-H/2.)))
      CLENON=CLENON/PI
      WRITE(6,3) N,FILON,CLENON
   16 CONTINUE
      WRITE(6,6)

C     SQUIRE"S GENERALIZED MIDPOINT(SEC.5.5)

      SQUIRE=0.0
      H=BIGT/FLOAT(N)
      R=2.0*SIN(X*H/2.)/X
      S=(2.0/(X*X))*(SIN(X*H/2.)-X*H/2.*COS(X*H/2.))
      DO 21 J=1,N
      U=(2.0*FLOAT(J)-1)*H/2.
      CALL FTSTAR(U,T,RSMF,USMF)
      D=(1.0+U*U)*(1.0+U*U)
      P=2.0*T*U
      Q=T*(1.0-U*U)
      PSMFDC=USMF*Q/D-(RSMF+EXP(-AMIN1(30.0,T)))*P/D
      USMFDC=-(RSMF+EXP(-AMIN1(30.0,T)))*Q/D-USMF*P/D
      SQUIRE=SQUIRE+R*(RSMF*COS(X*U)-USMF*SIN(X*U))-S*(RSMFDC*SIN(X*U)
     1     +USMFDC*COS(X*U))
   21 CONTINUE
      SQUIRE=SQUIRE/PI
      WRITE(6,103)
  103 FORMAT(2X,16HSQUIRES MIDPOINT)
      WRITE(6,5) SQUIRE
      WRITE(6,6)

C     STEHFEST-GAVER

      WRITE(6,105)
  105 FORMAT(2X,14HSTEHFEST-GAVER)
      DO 37 I=1,8
      NS=8+2*I
      NS2=NS/2
      FACT(1)=1.
         DO 34 J=2,NS
      FACT(J)=FACT(J-1)*FLOAT(J)
   34 CONTINUE
      TERM=(-1)**(NS2-1)*2.0/FACT(NS2-1)
      SUM=TERM*AP(T,ALOG(2.0)/X)
      DO 31 K=2,NS2
      TERM=-TERM*(FLOAT(K)**(NS2-1)/FLOAT(K-1)**(NS2-1))*FLOAT(2*K)*
     1FLOAT(2*K-1)*(NS2-K+1)/(FLOAT(K-1)*FLOAT(K-1)*FLOAT(K))
      SUM=SUM+TERM*AP(T,ALOG(2.0)*FLOAT(K)/X)
   31 CONTINUE

C     THE FIRST SUM IS COMPLETE

      DO 32 J=1,NS2
      IF(J.EQ.1) TERM=(-FLOAT(J))**(NS2 )*2.0/FACT(NS2-1)
      IF(J.EQ.1) SUM=SUM+TERM*AP(T,ALOG(2.0)*2.0/X)
      IF(J.EQ.1) GOTO 33
      IF(J.EQ.NS2) GOTO 36
      TERM=(-1)**(NS2 )*FLOAT(J)**(NS2-1)*FACT(2*J)/(FACT(J-1)*FACT(J-1
     1)*FACT(J)*FACT(NS2-J))
      SUM=SUM+TERM*AP(T,ALOG(2.0)*FLOAT(2*J)/X)
   33 J1=J+1
      DO 35 K=J1,NS2
      TERM=-TERM*(FLOAT(K)**(NS2-1)/FLOAT(K-1)**(NS2-1))*FLOAT(2*K)*
     1FLOAT(2*K-1)*FLOAT(NS2-K+1)/(FLOAT(K-1)*FLOAT(K-1)*FLOAT(K-J))
      SUM=SUM+TERM*AP(T,ALOG(2.0)*FLOAT(K+J)/X)
   35 CONTINUE
      GOTO 32
```

```
   36 SUM= (-1)**(NS2  )*FLOAT(J)**(NS2-1)*FACT(2*J)/(FACT(J-1)*FACT(J-1
     1 1)*FACT(J) /AP(T,ALOG(2.0)*FLOAT(NS)/X))+ SUM
   32 CONTINUE
      STEH=SUM*ALOG(2.0)/X
      PRESUM=FLOAT(NS)*ALOG(2.0)/(X*FACT(NS))
      N1=NS+1
      N2=2*NS
      DO 38 L=N1,N2
      PRESUM=PRESUM*FLOAT(L)
   38 CONTINUE
      GAV=AP(T,ALOG(2.0)*FLOAT(NS)/X)+AP(T,ALOG(2.0)*FLOAT(2*NS)/X)
      N3=NS-1
      DO 39 LL=1,N3
      GAV=GAV+(-1)**LL*FACT(NS)*AP(T,ALOG(2.0)*FLOAT(NS+LL)/X)/(FACT(LL)
     1 *FACT(NS-LL))
   39 CONTINUE
      GAV=GAV*PRESUM
      WRITE(6,3) NS,STEH,GAV
   37 CONTINUE
      WRITE(6,6)

C     FINARSSON

C     INSERT NEXT TEN  INSTRUCTIONS AND TWO EXTERNAL FUNCTIONS

      A=0.0
      B=BIGT
      W=X
      EPS=10.**(-6)
      MAX=10
      FPA=0.0
      GB=F(B,T)+EXP(-AMIN1(30.,T))
      FPB= GB *((1.0-B*B)*TAN( T *B/(1.+B*B)) + 2.*B)*(- T )/((1.+B*B)*
     1 (1.+B*B))
      FBA= - T  *( T  +2.0)
      FBB= GB *(- T /((1.+B*B)*(1.+B*B)))*(( T  *(1.-B*B)*(1.-B*B) +
     1 12.0*(1.+B*B)*(1.+B*B) - 8.*B*B*(1.+B*B) - 4.* T *B*B/((1.+B*B)*
     2 (1.+B*B)) -  TAN( T *B/(1.+B*B))*(2.*B+4.* T *B*(1.-B*B)/((1.+
     3 B*B)*(1.+B*B)) + 4.*B*(1.-B*B)/(1.+B*B)))
      LC=1
      LS=0
      ITIME=1
      FA=F(A,T)
      FB=F(B,T)
   10 N=1
      W1=ABS(W)
      TEMP=2.0*(B-A)*W1/PI
      IF(TEMP.GT.2.0) N=ALOG(TEMP)/0.693
      MXN=MAXO(MAX,N+1)
      COSA=COS(W1*A)
      SINA=SIN(W1*A)
      COSB=COS(W1*B)
      SINB=SIN(W1*B)
      H=(B-A)/FLOAT(2**N)
      NSTOP=2**N-1
      NST=1
      TMAX=0.2
      TMAXB=5.*TMAX
      IF(LS) 11,11,12
   11 LLS=2
      GOTO 13
   12 LLS=1
   13 IF(LC) 14,14,15
   14 LLC=2
      GOTO 17
   15 LLC=1
   17 CONTINUE
```

```
      SUMCOS=0.5*(FA*COSA+FB*COSB)
      SUMSIN=0.5*(FA*SINA+FB*SINB)
      M=1
   20 CONTINUE
      H2=H*H
      TETA=W1*H
      DO 65 I=1,NSTOP,NST
      XX=A+H*FLOAT(I)
      WX=W1*XX
      GOTO(50,50),LLS
   50 SUMSIN=SUMSIN+FF(XX,T)*SIN(WX)
   55 GOTO(60,65),LLC
   60 SUMCOS=SUMCOS+F(XX,T)*COS(WX)
   65 CONTINUE
      T2=TETA*TETA
      TEMP=1.0-SIN(0.5*TETA)**2/1.5
      IF(TETA-TMAX)70,70,75
   70 ALFA=TETA*(1.0-T2*(2.0/15.0-T2*(19.0/1680.0-T2*(13.0/25200.0-T2*
     1(293.0/19958400.0-T2*181.0/619164000.0)))))/12.0
      DELTA=-1.0/12.0+T2*(1.0/90.0              -T2*(5.0/12096.0-T2*
     1(1.0/129600.0-T2/11404800.0)))
      EPSIL=1.0-T2*(1.0/6.0-T2*(0.0125-T2*(17.0/30240.0-T2*(31.0/
     11814400.0-T2/2651120.0))))
      T3=T2
   72 BETA=TETA*H2*(1.0-T2/21.0*(1.0-T2*(1.0/48.0-T2*(1.0/3960.0-T3/
     11494208.0)))/180.0
      GOTO 80
   75 TEMP1=(0.5*TETA)**2
      TEMP2=SIN(0.5*TETA)**2/TEMP1
      TEMP3=SIN(TETA)/TETA
      ALFA=(TEMP-TEMP2*TEMP3)/TETA
      DELTA=(TEMP-TEMP2)/T2
      EPSIL=TEMP2*TEMP2
      IF(TETA-TMAX) 76,76,78
   76 T3=T2*(1.0-T2*(1.0/175.0-T2*(1.0/40800.0-T2/12209400.0)))
      GOTO 72
   78 BETA=(TEMP-TEMP3)/(TETA*W1*W1)
   80 GOTO(81,85),LLS
   81 TS=H*((BETA*FBB-ALFA*FB)*COSB+(ALFA*FA-BETA*FBA)*COSA+DELTA*H*(FPB
     1*SINB-FPA*SINA)+EPSIL*SUMSIN)/TEMP
      CALL ENOT2(PVTS,TS,EPS,S,LLS,M)
      LS=N
   85 GOTO(86,90),LLC
   86 TC=H*((ALFA*FB-3ETA*FBB)*SINB+(BETA*FBA-ALFA*FA)*SINA+DELTA*H*(FPB
     1*COSB-FPA*COSA)+EPSIL*SUMCOS)/TEMP
      CALL ENOT2(PVTC,TC,EPS,C,LLC,M)
      LC=N
   90 CONTINUE
      IF(LLC+LLS-3) 92,92,100
   92 N=N+1
      IF(N-MXN) 95,95,99
   95 H=0.5*H
      NST=2
      NSTOP=2**N
      M=M+1
      GO TO 20
   99 EPS=-EPS
  100 CONTINUE
      IF(ITIME.EQ.2) GO TO 200
      ITIME=2

   C     INSERT NEXT FOUR INSTRUCTIONS

      FPA=0.0
      FPB=FF(B,T)*((1.-B*B)/TAN(T*B/(1.+B*B))  -2.*B)*(+ T )/((1.+B*B)*
     1(1.+B*B))
      FBA=0.0
```

```
      FBB=FF(B,T)*(T/((1.+B*B)*(1.+B*B)))*((- T  *(1.-3*B)*(1.-B*B) -
   12.0*(1.+B*B)*(1.+B*B) + 8.*B*B*(1.+B*B) + 4.* T *B*B)/((1.+B*B)*
    2(1.+B*B)) -1./TAN( T *B/(1.+B*B))*(2.*B*4.* I *B*(1.-B*B)/((1.+
    3B*B)*(1.+B*B)) + 4.*B*(1.-B*B)/(1.+B*B)))
      LC=0
      LS=1
      FA=FF(A,T)
      FB=FF(B,T)
      GOTO 10
  200 EINAR=(C-S)/PI
      WRITE(6,106)
  106 FORMAT(2X,9HEINARSSON)
      WRITE(6,5) EINAR
      WRITE(6,6)
C
C     VAN DE VOOREN AND VAN LINDE EQNS 2.8 AND 3.6
C
      IP=IFIX(X*BIGI/(2.0*PI)) + 1
      PIX=PI/X
      BIGN=2.0*128.0*PIX
      SUM1=0.0
      SUM2=0.0
      SUM3=0.0
      SUM4=0.0
      SUM5=0.0
      SUM6=0.0
      SUM7=0.0
      SUM8=0.0
      DO 40 I=1,IP
      U=FLOAT(2*I-2)*PIX
      CALL FTSTAR(U,T,RSMF,USMF)
      SUM1=SUM1+RSMF
      U=FLOAT(2*I-1)*PIX
      CALL FTSTAR(U,T,RSMF,USMF)
      SUM1=SUM1-2.0*RSMF
      U=FLOAT(2*I)*PIX
      CALL FTSTAR(U,T,RSMF,USMF)
      SUM1=SUM1+RSMF
      U=(FLOAT(2*I) - 1.75)*PIX
      CALL FTSTAR(U,T,RSMF,USMF)
      SUM3=SUM3 + RSMF
      U=(FLOAT(2*I) - 1.25)*PIX
      CALL FTSTAR(U,T,RSMF,USMF)
      SUM3=SUM3 - RSMF
      U=(FLOAT(2*I) - 0.75)*PIX
      CALL FTSTAR(U,T,RSMF,USMF)
      SUM3=SUM3 - RSMF
      U=(FLOAT(2*I) - 0.25)*PIX
      CALL FTSTAR(U,T,RSMF,USMF)
      SUM3=SUM3 + RSMF
      U=(FLOAT(2*I) - 1.875)*PIX
      CALL FTSTAR(U,T,RSMF,USMF)
      SUM4=SUM4 + RSMF
      U=(FLOAT(2*I) - 1.125)*PIX
      CALL FTSTAR(U,T,PSMF,USMF)
      SUM4=SUM4 - RSMF
      U=(FLOAT(2*I) - 0.875)*PIX
      CALL FTSTAR(U,T,RSMF,USMF)
      SUM4=SUM4 - RSMF
      U=(FLOAT(2*I) - 0.125)*PIX
      CALL FTSTAR(U,T,RSMF,USMF)
      SUM4=SUM4 + RSMF
      U=(FLOAT(2*I) - 1.625)*PIX
      CALL FTSTAR(U,T,RSMF,USMF)
      SUM5=SUM5 + RSMF
      U=(FLOAT(2*I) - 1.375)*PIX
      CALL FTSTAR(U,T,RSMF,USMF)
```

```
      SUM5=SUM5 - RSMF
      U=(FLOAT(2*I) - 0.625)*PIX
      CALL FTSTAR(U,T,RSMF,USMF)
      SUM5=SUM5 - RSMF
      U=(FLOAT(2*I) - 0.375)*PIX
      CALL FTSTAR(U,T,RSMF,USMF)
      SUM5=SUM5 + RSMF
      U=(FLOAT(2*I)-1.5)*PIX
      CALL FTSTAR(U,T,RSMF,USMF)
      SUM2=SUM2+USMF
      U=(FLOAT(2*I)-0.5)*PIX
      CALL FTSTAR(U,T,RSMF,USMF)
      SUM2=SUM2-USMF
      U=(FLOAT(2*I) - 1.75)*PIX
      CALL FTSTAR(U,T,RSMF,USMF)
      SUM6=SUM6 + USMF
      U=(FLOAT(2*I) - 1.25)*PIX
      CALL FTSTAR(U,T,RSMF,USMF)
      SUM6=SUM6 + USMF
      U=(FLOAT(2*I) - 0.75)*PIX
      CALL FTSTAR(U,T,RSMF,USMF)
      SUM6=SUM6 - USMF
      U=(FLOAT(2*I) - 0.25)*PIX
      CALL FTSTAR(U,T,RSMF,USMF)
      SUM6=SUM6 - USMF
      U=(FLOAT(2*I) - 1.875)*PIX
      CALL FTSTAR(U,T,RSMF,USMF)
      SUM7=SUM7 + USMF
      U=(FLOAT(2*I) - 1.125)*PIX
      CALL FTSTAR(U,T,RSMF,USMF)
      SUM7=SUM7 + USMF
      U=(FLOAT(2*I) - 0.875)*PIX
      CALL FTSTAR(U,T,RSMF,USMF)
      SUM7=SUM7 - USMF
      U=(FLOAT(2*I) - 0.125)*PIX
      CALL FTSTAR(U,T,RSMF,USMF)
      SUM7=SUM7 - USMF
      U=(FLOAT(2*I) - 1.625)*PIX
      CALL FTSTAR(U,T,RSMF,USMF)
      SUM8=SUM8 + USMF
      U=(FLOAT(2*I) - 1.375)*PIX
      CALL FTSTAR(U,T,RSMF,USMF)
      SUM8=SUM8 + USMF
      U=(FLOAT(2*I) - 0.625)*PIX
      CALL FTSTAR(U,T,RSMF,USMF)
      SUM8=SUM8 - USMF
      U=(FLOAT(2*I) - 0.375)*PIX
      CALL FTSTAR(U,T,RSMF,USMF)
      SUM8=SUM8 - USMF
   40 CONTINUE
      SQ=SQRT(2.0)
      SUM1=2.0*(6.0+SQ-16.0*SQ/PI)*SUM1/(PI*X)+4.0*(1.0+3.0*SQ-16.0/PI)
     1   *SUM3/(PI*X)+8.0*(8.0*SQ/PI-2.0-SQ)*SUM4/(PI*X)+8.0*((16.0-8.*
     2 SQ)/PI-SQ)*SUM5/(PI*X)
      U=BIGN
      CALL FTSTAR(U,T,RSMF,USMF)
      PI2=PI*PI
      PI3=PI*PI*PI
      PI4=PI*PI*PI*PI
      SUM2=(3.0*PI4+6.0*PI3-560.0*PI2-2304.0*PI+12238.0)*(ZERORD-USMF)/
     1   (3.0*PI4*X)+4.0*(25.0*PI3-88.0*PI2-1920.0*PI+6144.0)*SUM2/(3.0*
     2   PI4*X)+8.0*(3.0*PI3-75.0*PI2-768.0*PI+3072.0)*SUM6/(PI4*X)+32.0*
     3   (-PI3+52.0*PI2+336.0*PI-1536.0)*SUM7/(3.0*PI4*X)+32.0*(-3.0*PI3+
     4   28.0*PI2+432.0*PI-1536.0)*SUM8/(3.0*PI4*X)
      SMLF=(SUM1-SUM2)/PI
      WRITE(6,108)
```

```
  108 FORMAT(2X,10HVAN VOOREN)
      WRITE(6,3) IP,SMLF
      WRITE(6,6)
C     THE EXACT VALUE

      S=3.75/(2.0*SQRT(X*T))
      BI=-.00420059
      BI=BI*S+.01787654
      BI=BI*S-.02895312
      BI=BI*S+.02282957
      BI=BI*S-.01031555
      BI=BI*S+.00163801
      BI=BI*S-.00362018
      BI=BI*S-.03988024
      BI=BI*S+.39894228
      BI=T*EXP(2.0*SQRT(T*X)-X-T)*BI/(SQRT(2.0*(T*X)**1.5))
      WRITE(6,110)
  110 FORMAT(2X,11HEXACT VALUE)
      WRITE(6,5) BI
      STOP
      END



      FUNCTION F(X,T)
      F=EXP(-AMIN1(30.0,T-T/(1.+X*X)))*COS(T*X/(1.+X*X))-EXP(-AMIN1(30.,
     1 T))
      RETURN
      END



      FUNCTION FF(X,T)
      FF=-EXP(-AMIN1(30.,T-T/(1.+X*X)))*SIN(T*X/(1.+X*X))
      RETURN
      END



      FUNCTION AP(T,X)
      AP=EXP(-AMIN1(30.,T)*X/(1.+X))-EXP(-AMIN1(30.,T))
      RETURN
      END



      SUBROUTINE FTSTAR(U,T,RSMF,USMF)
      BETR=1./(1.+U*U)
      BETI=-U/(1.+U*U)
      RSMF=EXP(-AMIN1(30.,T-T*BETR))*COS(T*BETI)-EXP(-AMIN1(30.,T))
      USMF=EXP(-AMIN1(30.,T-T*BETR))*SIN(T*BETI)
      RETURN
      END



      SUBROUTINE ALBEGA(TH,AL,BE,GA)
      IF(TH.LE.0.167) GO TO 1
      AL=(TH*TH+TH*SIN(TH)*COS(TH)-2.0*SIN(TH)*SIN(TH))/(TH*TH*TH)
      BE=2.0*(TH*(1.0+COS(TH)*COS(TH))-2.0*SIN(TH)*COS(TH))/(TH*TH*TH)
      GA=4.0*(SIN(TH)-TH*COS(TH))/(TH*TH*TH)
      GO TO 2
    1 AL=2.0*TH*TH*TH/45.0-2.0*TH**5/315.0+2.0*TH**7/4725.0
      BE=2.0/3.0+2.0*TH*TH/15.0+4.0*TH**4/105.0+2.0*TH**6/567.0
      GA=4.0/3.0-2.0*TH*TH/15.0+TH**4/210.0-TH**6/11340.0
    2 RETURN
      END
```

```
SUBROUTINE FNDT2(PREVOT,QUANT,EPS,VALUE,L,M)
DIMENSION PREVOT(7),RICH(7)
DATA RICH(1)/ 0.0/,RICH(2)/15.0/,RICH(3)/63.0/,RICH(4)/255.0/,
1    RICH(5)/1023.0/,RICH(6)/4095.0/,RICH(7)/16383.0/
TEMP2=PREVOT(1)
PREVOT(1)=QUANT
TEMP1=QUANT
IF(M.EQ.1) GOTO 30
20 PEPS=EPS*(1.0+ABS(QUANT))
DO 23 K=2,M
DIFF=TEMP1-TEMP2
IF(ABS(DIFF)-PEPS) 25,25,22
22 IF(K.EQ.8) GOTO 30
TEMP1=TEMP1+DIFF/RICH(K)
TEMP2=PREVOT(K)
PREVOT(K)=TEMP1
23 CONTINUE
GOTO 30
25 L=2
30 VALUE=TEMP1
RETURN
END
```

GETUWT

This is a general program for the calculation of $U(w, t)$, the probability of insurance company survival to the end of an interval of time during which t claims are expected. If the formula for $p_n(t)$ is Poisson, negative binomial or generalized Waring (see Chapter 2) and that for $b(y)$ is exponential or inverse normal (Chapter 2) the only punching required is the parameters specified in 10 comment cards in the 'main' progam and a possibly different value for L from 4 if IPTYPE = 3. The formula for $U(w, t)$ is (4.1) and t proceeds by unit steps. When IPTYPE is 1 or 2 (4.6) is used for $U(0, t)$. On the other hand when $p_n(t)$ is generalized Waring $U(0, t)$ must be found by solving an integral equation using subroutine INTEQN. For this purpose quarter-unit steps in t have been used.

We believe that N should never be chosen less than 1024 while BIGT should be about 30 π, 40 π or, even, 50 π.

The following recommendations are made to ensure the successful use of GETUWT:

(1) The print-out of the six integrands (omitting the sine and cosine factors) at $t = 1$ and $t = K$ (the highest value), respectively, indicates whether BIGT has been chosen large enough. Relation (3.12) serves as a guide.
(2) The run of values of $F(\cdot, t)$, $f(\cdot, t)$ and $U(0, t)$, for given t, as the number of trapezoidal panels is successively doubled should indicate whether N has been chosen large enough. At least two successive N-values should produce the same function value to the required number of decimals. The output shows the values of $F(w + \pi_1 t, t)$, $f(w + \pi_1 t, t)$ and $U(0, t)$ for 2, 4, 8, ... trapezoidal panels using (3.10), and the first of these functions has been 'checked' on the extreme right of the output using (3.11). These latter values are *not* applied in the evaluation of (4.1).

(3) For given K and with $N = 2048$ the execution time required for the six programmed pairs of IPTYPE, IBTYPE values are (on a CDC 6500) in the ratios: 1, 1 = 1.0, 1, 2 = 1.48, 2, 1 = 1.13, 2, 2 = 1.58, 3, 1 = 5.10, 3, 2 = 6.89. Execution is otherwise proportional to the K-values chosen; on a CDC 6500 the above unit was equal to 29.5 seconds for $K = 5$ and was reduced to 16 seconds when $N = 1024$.

```
PROGRAM GETUWT(INPUT,OUTPUT,TAPE5 =INPUT,TAPE6=OUTPUT)
DIMENSION BIGF(25),SMLF(25),U0(25),UW(25),HH(25),UINF(25),A(25)
WRITE(6,11)
PI=3.14159265
C   N IS THE NUMBER OF TRAPEZOIDAL PANELS, PI1 IS THE LOADED PREMIUM,
C   K IS THE NUMBER OF T-VALUES, W IS THE RISK RESERVE, BIGT IS THE
C   UPPER LIMIT OF INTEGRATION IN LIEU OF INFINITY, HB IS THE NEGATIVE
C   BINOMIAL INDEX WHEN USED, AND AW,BW, AND CW ARE THE WARING PARAMETERS
C   (AW*BW/CW = 1.0 IF MEAN IS TO BE T.        BW*T MUST BE INTEGRAL)
C   BEFORE MULTIPLICATION BY T. IPTYPE=1,2,3 ARE THE POISSON, NEGATIVE
C   BINOMIAL AND GENERALIZED WARING CLAIM NUMBER DISTRIBUTIONS,
C   RESPECTIVELY. IBTYPE=1,2 ARE THE EXPONENTIAL AND INVERSE NORMAL
C   CLAIM SIZE DISTRIBUTIONS, RESPECTIVELY, WITH XLAM=LAMBDA.L=NO. OF
C   T-VALUES IN UNIT TIME.
N=2048
PI1=1.1
K=5
BIGT=44.0*PI
HB=20.
AW=2.0
BW=4.0
CW=8.0
XLAM=2.20408
IPTYPE=3
IBTYPE=2
IF(IPTYPE.EQ.3) L=4
IF(IPTYPE.EQ.3) W=0.0
IF(IPTYPE.EQ.3) K=L*K
IF(IPTYPE.EQ.3) GO TO 8
5 L=1
W=10.0
IF(IPTYPE.EQ.3) K=K1
CALL GETBGF(K,N,BIGT,W,PI1,HB,AW,BW,CW,XLAM,IPTYPE,IBTYPE,BIGF,
1SMLF,U0,L)
WRITE(6,2)
WRITE(6,1) BIGF
WRITE(6,1) SMLF
WRITE(6,1) U0
WRITE(6,10)
CALL REPSIM(K,PI1,BIGF,SMLF,U0,UW,L)
WRITE(6,3)
WRITE(6,1) UW
GO TO 9
8 CALL GETBGF(K,N,BIGT,W,PI1,HB,AW,BW,CW,XLAM,IPTYPE,IBTYPE,BIGF,
1SMLF,U0,L)
DO 7 J=1,K
HH(J)=-SMLF(J)*PI1
7 CONTINUE
H=1.0/FLOAT(L)
NN=K
UI0=1.0
HH0=0.0
CALL INTEQN(BIGF,PI1,H,NN,HH,UI0,HH0,UINF)
K1=K/L
DO 6 J=1,K1
JL=J*L
U0(J)=UINF(JL)
```

```
   6 CONTINUE
     WRITE(6,4)
     WRITE(6,1)  (U0(M),M=1,K1)
     WRITE(6,10)
     GO TO 5
   1 FORMAT(10E13.5)
   2 FORMAT(2X,32HFINAL VALUES OF BIGF,SMLF AND U0)
   3 FORMAT(2X,12HVALUES OF UW)
   4 FORMAT(2X,24HVALUES OF U0 FROM INTEQN)
  10 FORMAT(1H0)
  11 FORMAT(1H1)
   9 STOP
     END

     SUBROUTINE GETBGF(K,N,BIGT,W,PI1,HB,AW,BW,CW,XLAM,IPTYPE,IBTYPE,
    1BIGF,SMLF,U0,L)
     DIMENSION BIGF(K),SMLF(K),U0(K)
   5 FORMAT(6E13.6)
     DO 8 IT=1,K
     T=FLOAT(IT)/FLOAT(L)
     X=W+PI1*T
     SUMMBF = -T
     SUMMU0 = -T-PI1*T/2.0
     CALL RANILT(PI1,0.0,T,HB,AW,BW,CW,XLAM,IPTYPE,IBTYPE,RSMF,USMF,
    1RBGF,UBGF,RU0,UJ0)
     ZERORD = RSMF
     U=BIGT
     CALL RANILT(PI1, U ,T,HB,AW,BW,CW,XLAM,IPTYPE,IBTYPE,RSMF,USMF,
    1RBGF,UBGF,RU0,UJ0)
     IF(IT.EQ.1.OR.IT.EQ.K) WRITE(6,9)
     IF(IT.EQ.1.OR.IT.EQ.K) WRITE(6,5) RSMF,USMF,RBGF,UBGF,RU0,UU0
     SUMMSF = (ZERORD+RSMF*COS(X*U) - USMF*SIN(X*U))*BIGT/2.0
     SUMMBF = (SUMMBF + RBGF*COS(X*J) - UBGF*SIN(X*U))*BIGT/2.0
     SUMMU0 = (SUMMU0 + RU0*COS(PI1*T*U) - UU0*SIN(PI1*T*U))*BIGT/2.0
     CALL DOUBLE(PI1,N,BIGT,T,X,HB,AW,BW,CW,XLAM,IPTYPE,IBTYPE,SUMMSF,
    1SUMMBF,SUMMU0,BIGFF,SMLFF,U0T)
     BIGF(IT) = BIGFF
     SMLF(IT) = SMLFF
     IF(IPTYPE.EQ.3) GO TO 8
     U0(IT)=U0T
   8 CONTINUE
   9 FORMAT(2X,51HVALUES OF REAL AND IMAGINARY INTEGRANDS AT T=1 OR K)
     RETURN
     END

     SUBROUTINE DOUBLE(PI1,N,BIGT,T,X,HB,AW,BW,CW,XLAM,IPTYPE,IBTYPE,
    1SUMMSF,SUMMBF,SUMMU0,BIGFF,SMLFF,U0T)
     PI = 3.14159265
     U=BIGT
     CALL RANILT(PI1,U,T,HB,AW,BW,CW,XLAM,IPTYPE,IBTYPE,RSMF,USMF,RBGF,
    1UBGF,RU0,UU0)
     SUMM11=(-T+RBGF*COS(X*U))*BIGT/2.0
     NN = 1
     WRITE(6,6)
   2 NN = 2*NN
     NN1 = NN/2
     H = BIGT/FLOAT(NN)
     SUMSF = 0.0
     SUMBF = 0.0
     SUMU0 = 0.0
     SUM11=0.0
     DO 1 I=1,NN1
     U = FLOAT(2*I-1)*H
     CALL RANILT(PI1,U,T,HB,AW,BW,CW,XLAM,IPTYPE,IBTYPE,RSMF,USMF,RBGF,
    1UBGF,RU0,UU0)
     SUMSF = SUMSF + 2.0*H*(RSMF*COS(X*U)-USMF*SIN(X*U))
     SUMBF = SUMBF + 2.0*H*(RBGF*COS(X*U)-UBGF*SIN(X*U))
     SUM11=SUM11+2.0*H*RBGF*COS(X*U)
     IF(IPTYPE.EQ.3) GO TO 1
```

```
      SUMU0 = SUMU0 + 2.0*H*(RU0*COS(PI1*T*U)-UU0*SIN(PI1*T*U))
    1 CONTINUE
      SUMMSF = (SUMMSF + SUMSF)/2.0
      SUMMBF = (SUMMBF + SUMBF)/2.0
      SUMM11=(SUMM11+SUM11)/2.0
      BIGFF = SUMMBF/PI +0.5 + H*X/(2.0*PI)
      SMLFF = SUMMSF/PI
      IF(IPTYPE.EQ.3) U0T=0.0
      IF(IPTYPE.EQ.3) GO TO 7
      SUMMU0 = (SUMMU0 + SUMU0)/2.0
      U0T = SUMMU0/PI + 0.5 + H*PI1*T/(2.0*PI)
    7 BIGF11=2.0*SUMM11/PI + 1.0
      WRITE(6,3) NN,BIGFF,SMLFF,U0T,BIGF11
    3 FORMAT(2X,I5,5X,3E13.6,50X,E13.5)
      IF(NN.EQ.N) GO TO 4
      GO TO 2
    4 WRITE(6,5)
    5 FORMAT(1H0)
    6 FORMAT(2X,42HVALUES OF BIGF,SMLF AND U0 AT SUCCESSIVE T)
      RETURN
      END

      SUBROUTINE RANILT(PI1,U,T,HB,AW,BW,CW,XLAM,IPTYPE,IBTYPE,RSMF,
     1USMF,RBGF,UBGF,RU0,UU0)
      PTU=PI1*T*U
      IF(IBTYPE-1) 1,1,2
    1 P=1.0/(1.0+U*U)
      Q=-U/(1.0+U*U)
      GO TO 3
    2 AA=(1.0+4.0*U*U/(XLAM*XLAM))**0.25
      BB=ATAN2(2.0*U,XLAM)/2.0
      P=EXP(XLAM-XLAM*AA*COS(BB))*COS(XLAM*AA*SIN(BB))
      Q=-EXP(XLAM-XLAM*AA*COS(BB))*SIN(XLAM*AA*SIN(BB))
    3 IF(IPTYPE-2) 4,5,6
    4 P0=EXP(-AMIN1(30.0,T))
      USMF=EXP(-AMIN1(30.0,T-T*P))*SIN(T*Q)
      RSMF=EXP(-AMIN1(30.0,T-T*P))*COS(T*Q) - P0
      IF(U.EQ.0.0) GO TO 10
      GO TO 7
    5 G=((1.0+T/HB-T*P/HB)**2 + (T*Q/HB)**2)**(-HB/2.0)
      BIGH=ATAN2( T*Q,HB+T-T*P)*HB
      CU=G*COS(BIGH)
      DU=G*SIN(BIGH)
      P0=(HB/(T+HB))**HB
      RSMF=CU-P0
      USMF=DU
      IF(U.EQ.0.0) GO TO 10
      GO TO 7
    6 R=SQRT(P*P+Q*Q)
      S=ATAN2(Q,P)
C     B IS SUPPOSED AN INTEGER
      A=AW*T
      B=BW*T
      C=CW*T+1.0
      CALL WARING(A,B,C,R,S,WARG1,WARG2,XMULT)
      P0=XMULT
      RSMF=WARG1-P0
      USMF=WARG2
      IF(U.EQ.0.0) GO TO 10
    7 RBGF=USMF/U
      UBGF=-(RSMF+P0)/U
      RU0=((1.0-COS(PTU))*UBGF + SIN(PTU)*RBGF)/PTU
      IF(IPTYPE.EQ.3) UU0=0.0
      IF(IPTYPE.EQ.3) GO TO 10
      UU0=(SIN(PTU)*UBGF-(1.0-COS(PTU))*RBGF)/PTU
   10 RETURN
      END

      SUBROUTINE WARING(A,B,C,R,S,WARG1,WARG2,XMULT)
      IB=IFIX(B)-1
```

```
      C=C+A+B
      TOP=C-A-B
      BOT=C-B
      DO 1 J=1,IB
      TOP=TOP*(C-A-B+FLOAT(J))
      BOT=BOT*(C-B+FLOAT(J))
    1 CONTINUE
      XMULT=TOP/BOT
      SUM1=1.0
      SUM2=1.0
      TERM=1.0
      DO 2 J=1,100
      TERM=TERM*(A+FLOAT(J-1))*(B+FLOAT(J-1))/((C+FLOAT(J-1))*FLOAT(J))
      TERM1=TERM*R**J*COS(FLOAT(J)*S)
      TERM2=TERM*R**J*SIN(FLOAT(J)*S)
      SUM1=SUM1+TERM1
      SUM2=SUM2+TERM2
      IF(TERM1*XMULT.LT.1.0E-6) GO TO 3
    2 CONTINUE
    3 WARG1=XMULT*SUM1
      WARG2=XMULT*SUM2
      RETURN
      END


      SUBROUTINE REPSIM(K,PI1,BIGF,SMLF,U0,UW,L)
      DIMENSION BIGF(1),SMLF(1),U0(1),UW(1)
      TSTEP=1.0/FLOAT(L)
      ETA1=PI1
      UW(1) = BIGF(1) - ETA1*SMLF(1)*TSTEP*0.5
      UW(2) = BIGF(2) - ETA1*(SMLF(2)+4.0*U0(1)*SMLF(1))*TSTEP/3.0
      UW(3) = BIGF(3) - ETA1*3.0*(SMLF(3)+3.0*U0(1)*SMLF(2)+3.0*U0(2)*
     1       SMLF(1))*TSTEP/8.0
      DO 25 IT=4,K
      IT1 = IT-1
      IF((IT/2)*2.EQ.IT)UW(IT) = SMLF(IT)
      IF((IT/2)*2.NE.IT) UW(IT) = 9.0*(3.0*U0(IT1)*SMLF(1) + 3.0*U0(
     1       IT1-1)*SMLF(2) + U0(IT1-2)*SMLF(3))/8.0 + SMLF(IT)
     2     - U0(IT1-2)*SMLF(3)
      DO 24 J=1,IT1
      IF((IT/2)*2.EQ.IT.AND.(J/2)*2.NE.J) UW(IT) = UW(IT) + 4.0*U0(J)
     1       *SMLF(IT-J)
      IF((IT/2)*2.EQ.IT.AND.(J/2)*2.EQ.J) UW(IT) = UW(IT)+2.0*U0(J)*
     1       SMLF(IT-J)
      IF((IT/2)*2.NE.IT.AND.J.GT.IT-3) GO TO 24
      IF((IT/2)*2.NE.IT.AND.(J/2)*2.NE.J) UW(IT) = UW(IT)+4.0*U0(J)*
     1       SMLF(IT-J)
      IF((IT/2)*2.NE.IT.AND.(J/2)*2.EQ.J) UW(IT) = UW(IT)+2.0*U0(J)*
     1       SMLF(IT-J)
   24 CONTINUE
      UW(IT) = BIGF(IT) - ETA1*UW(IT)*TSTEP/3.0
   25 CONTINUE
      RETURN
      END


      SUBROUTINE INTEQN(A,PI1,H,NN,HH,U0,HH0,UINF)
      DIMENSION UINF(1),HH(1),A(1)
      TSTEP=H
      UINF(1)=(A(1)+H*U0*HH(1)/2.0)/(1.0-H*HH0/2.0)
      UINF(2)=( A(2)   +H*(4.0*UINF(1)*HH(1) +     U0  *HH(2))/3.)/(1.-
     1H*HH0/3.0)
      UINF(3)=(   A(3)  + 3.*H*(3.*UINF(2)*HH(1)+3.*UINF(1)*HH(2)+
     1 U0 *HH(3))/9.)/(1.-3.*H*HH0/8.0)
      DO 25 IT=4,NN
      IT1 = IT-1
      IF((IT/2)*2.EQ.IT)UINF(IT)=A(IT)*3.0/H + U0*HH(IT)
      IF((IT/2)*2.NE.IT)UINF(IT)= 9.0*(3.0*HH(IT1)*UINF(1) + 3.0*HH(
     1       IT1-1)*UINF(2) + HH(IT1-2)*UINF(3))/8.0
     2     - HH(IT1-2)*UINF(3) +     A   *(3.0/TSTEP)+9.*HH(IT)*U0/8.
      DO 24 J=1,IT1
      IF((IT/2)*2.EQ.IT.AND.(J/2)*2.NE.J)UINF(IT)=UINF(IT)+ 4.0*HH(J)
```

```
   1          *UINF(IT-J)
      IF((IT/2)*2.EQ.IT.AND.(J/2)*2.EQ.J)UINF(IT)=UINF(IT)+2.*HH(J)*
   1              UINF(IT-J)
      IF((IT/2)*2.NE.IT.AND.J.GT.IT-3) GO TO 24
      IF((IT/2)*2.NE.IT.AND.(J/2)*2.NE.J)UINF(IT)=UINF(IT)+4.*HH(J)*
   1              UINF(IT-J)
      IF((IT/2)*2.NE.IT.AND.(J/2)*2.EQ.J)UINF(IT)=UINF(IT)+2.*HH(J)*
   1              UINF(IT-J)
  24 CONTINUE
     UINF(IT)=UINF(IT)*TSTFP/(3.*(1.-H*HH0/3.0))
  25 CONTINUE
     RETURN
     END
```

GETBRM

This is an alternative method of inverting the Laplace transforms of the functions involved in (4.1) which Seal (1974) reports to break down for $t > 1000$. When used for the Poisson/exponential situation the inversion is accurate to at least five decimals up to $t = 40$ (Seal, 1974, Table 2). However the quadrature of the integral in (4.1) utilizing integer τ-values results in the loss of one, or even two, decimals. The complications introduced by the generalized Waring form for $p_n(t)$ have been bypassed by excluding this option.

The inversion formula that is approximated is

$$\frac{1}{2\pi i} \int_{c-i\infty}^{c+i\infty} e^p \frac{F(p)}{p} \, dp \simeq \sum_{j=1}^{24} A_j F(p_j)$$

(Krylov and Skoblya, 1969, Chapter 2) where 30 significant figures of $A_j = a + ib$, say, and p_j are given in Stroud and Secrest (1966) and used in the program.

The Laplace transforms of $F(x, t)$ and $f(x, t)$ are, respectively, $\psi_t(s)$ and $s\psi_t(s) - F(0, t)$ (as derived just before (3.14)). As stated, we have limited this program to mixed Poisson input $p_n(t)$ with infinitely divisible mixing distribution so that (4.6) applies and the Laplace transform of $U(0, t)$ is

$$\frac{1 - e^{-s(1+\eta)t}}{s(1 + \eta)t} \, \psi_t(s)$$

(as in (4.7)). To apply the foregoing integration formula we have to identify $F(p)$ in each case.

We have

$$e^{sx} \psi_t(s)ds = e^p \frac{\dfrac{p}{x} \psi_t\left(\dfrac{p}{x}\right)}{p} \, dp$$

implying

$$F(p) = \frac{p}{x} \psi_t\left(\frac{p}{x}\right)$$

$$e^{sx} \{s\psi_t(s) - F(0, t)\}ds = e^p \frac{\left(\dfrac{p}{x}\right)^2 \psi\left(\dfrac{p}{x}\right) - \dfrac{p}{x} F(0, t)}{p} \, dp$$

implying

$$F(p) = \left(\frac{p}{x}\right)^2 \psi\left(\frac{p}{x}\right) - \frac{p}{x} F(0, t)$$

and, with $x \equiv (1 + \eta)t$,

$$e^{sx} \frac{1 - e^{-sx}}{sx} \psi_t(s)ds = e^p \frac{1 - e^{-p}}{p} \frac{\frac{p}{x} \psi\left(\frac{p}{x}\right)}{p} dp$$

implying

$$F(p) = \frac{1 - e^{-p}}{p} \frac{p}{x} \psi\left(\frac{p}{x}\right)$$

If we write $F(p) = R + iS$ and associate $R = iS$ with $a - ib$

$$\Sigma AF(p) = \Sigma\left[(a + ib)(R + iS) + (a - ib)(R - iS)\right]$$
$$= 2\Sigma(aR - bS)$$

One further point should be mentioned. The Laplace transform of $F(x, t) - F(0, t)$ is $\psi_t(s) - 1/s \, F(0, t)$. If this last expression is substituted for $\psi_t(s)$ in the derivation of $F(p)$ for $U(0, t)$ we find

$$F(p) = \frac{1 - e^{-p}}{p}\left\{\frac{p}{x} \psi\left(\frac{p}{x}\right) - F(0, t)\right\}$$

remembering, of course, that $F(0, t)$ has to be added to $U(0, t)$ when the inversion has been effected. This strange subtraction–addition (which is in the following program) turned out to improve substantially the accuracy of the inversion for $t = 1, 2, 3, \ldots$ in the Poisson/exponential case where it can be checked. If the reader is dubious of its justification he has only to:

(i) remove the instruction $R = R - P0$ in subroutine BROM, and
(ii) delete $P0$ in the instruction U01(IT) shortly thereafter.

The program is to be used in the same manner as GETUWT by inserting the values of K, ETA (the risk loading on the pure premium), and W in the 'main' program, and in subroutine BROM as many of HB and XLAM as are needed for the chosen values of IPTYPE (1 or 2) and IBTYPE (1 or 2).

```
    PROGRAM GETBRM(INPUT,OUTPUT,TAPE5=INPUT,TAPE6=OUTPUT)
    DIMENSION UW(25),A(25),B(25),C(25),D(25),E(25),F(25),G(25)
    DOUBLE PRECISION A,B,C,D,E,F,G
    WRITE(6,11)
 11 FORMAT(1H1)
    K=5
    ETA=0.1
    W = 10.0
```

```
      CALL BROM(ETA, K,W,UW,A,B,C,D,E,F,G)
      STOP
      END


      SUBROUTINE BROM(ETA,ITOP,W,UW,BIGF,SMLF,U0,SMLFU0,SMLF1,BIGF1,
     1        U01)
      DIMENSION BIGF(ITOP),SMLF(ITOP),U0(ITOP),SMLFU0(ITOP),UW(ITOP)
      DIMENSION SMLF1(ITOP),BIGF1(ITOP),U01(ITOP)
      DIMENSION A(12),B(12),C(12),U(12)
      DOUBLE PRECISION A,B,C,U,UU,CC,R,S,R1,S1,R2,SMLF1,BIGF1,U01,T1
      DOUBLE PRECISION X1,P0
      TSTEP = 1.0
      ETA1 = 1.0 + ETA
      PI1=ETA1
      HB=2.0
      XLAM=2.20408
      IPTYPE=2
      IBTYPE=1
      IGAUSS=12
      DATA A/  -.92026241939286413054057247411D 11,
     1          .21159039115918247805415180795D 12,
     2         -.20574113755725574515486978404D 12,
     3          .12606056725559900597471558840D 12,
     4         -.51892363503397770711740199035D 11,
     5          .14255196516711712979751394698D 11,
     6         -.24762665373229200972793986496D 10,
     7          .23817597478873657322777153931D 09,
     8         -.80303094417976735619197484733D 07,
     9         -.30749455714443445397061861053D 06,
     9          .16467703376511226337972123222D 05,
     9         -.32223518977110381055350698564D 02/

      DATA B/   .77053877325448305822723136329D 12,
     1         -.56318663053761873507198539611D 12,
     2          .29534113216074563994601210119D 12,
     2         -.10581343296915512357730145734D 12,
     3          .22655330180457451033073643393D 11,
     4         -.13247141391464445257830093078D 10,
     5         -.68997441956837328076752020329D 09,
     6          .20081389659922686066391916306D 09,
     7         -.22158000278926464727887260640D 08,
     8          .92837833789110772717387941456D 06,
     9         -.57328206872886937376340177033D 04,
     9         -.65580676094791346080220259331D 02/

      DATA C/   .31436508082593193233786652031D 02,
     1          .31178157979731876194858047102D 02,
     2          .30656667740085775535056514760D 02,
     3          .29862047033353357579852883444D 02,
     4          .28777980912984835019841423791D 02,
     5          .27380056163539517516603087179D 02,
     6          .25632416591806091103947293261D 02,
     7          .23481770451025574441935080124D 02,
     8          .20845559883320797499202965354D 02,
     9          .17585929148066398417328283098D 02,
     9          .13437933384625530924729768869D 02,
     9          .77249240182072952245226799326D 01/

      DATA U/   .17061669621803822207294750504D 01,
     1          .51213645226617905333767779850D 01,
     2          .85453622364241797274479117545D 01,
```

```
 3            .11984762166348554180430292356D 02,
 4            .15447415288891283162950392948D 02,
 5            .18943270721199922806528681689D 02,
 6            .22485749859954908015024029695D 02,
 7            .26094197736323006925196021404D 02,
 8            .29798753623525798541795714316D 02,
 9            .33651484406379268492729821181D 02,
 9            .37757812928792822795687289970D 02,
 9            .42407449314134539739224699489D 02/


      DO 30 IT = 1,ITOP
      T1  = FLOAT(IT)*TSTEP
      X1 = W + ETA1*T1
      SMLF1(IT) = 0.0D0
      BIGF1(IT) = 0.0D0
      U01(IT) = 0.0D0
      DO 31 J=1,IGAUSS
      UU = U(J)/X1
      CC = C(J)/X1
      CALL RANL(PI1,CC,UU,T1,HB,XLAM,IPTYPE,IBTYPE,R,S,P0)
      BIGF1(IT)= BIGF1(IT)+ A(J)*R - B(J)*S
                 R1= R*CC - S*UU - CC*P0
                 S1= R*UU + S*CC - UU*P0
                 SMLF1(IT)= SMLF1(IT) + A(J)*R1 - B(J)*S1
      UU = U(J)/(ETA1*T1)
      CC = C(J)/(ETA1*T1)
      CALL RANL(PI1,CC,UU,T1,HB,XLAM,IPTYPE,IBTYPE,R,S,P0)
      R=R-P0
      R1 = (1.0-DEXP(-C(J))*DCOS(U(J)))/(C(J)**2 + U(J)**2)
      R2 = DEXP(-C(J))*DSIN(U(J))/(C(J)**2 + U(J)**2)
      U01(IT)=U01(IT)+A(J)*(R*(C(J)*R1+U(J)*R2)-S*(C(J)*R2-U(J)*R1))
     1       - B(J)*(R*(C(J)*R2 - U(J)*R1) + S*(C(J)*R1 + U(J)*R2))
 31   CONTINUE
 35                SMLF1(IT) = 2.0*SMLF1(IT)
      BIGF1(IT)= 2.0*BIGF1(IT)
      U01(IT) = 2.0*U01(IT) + P0
 30   CONTINUE
      DO 32 I=1,ITOP
      SMLF(I) = SNGL(SMLF1(I))
      BIGF(I) = SNGL(BIGF1(I))
 32   CONTINUE
      DO 33 I=1,ITOP
      U0(I) = SNGL(U01(I))
 33   CONTINUE
 34   CONTINUE
      WRITE(6,90)
 90   FORMAT(10X,24HVALUES OF SMALL F(W+T,T))
      WRITE(6,10) SMLF
      WRITE(6,11)
      WRITE(6,91)
 91   FORMAT(10X,21HVALUES OF BIGF(W+T,T))
      WRITE(6,10) BIGF
      WRITE(6,11)
      WRITE(6,92)
 92   FORMAT(10X,16HVALUES OF U(0,T))
      WRITE(6,10) U0
      WRITE(6,11)
      CALL REPSIM(ITOP,PI1,BIGF,SMLF,U0,UW)
      WRITE(6,93)
 93   FORMAT(10X,16HVALUES OF U(W,T))
      WRITE(6,10) UW
```

```
10 FORMAT(10E13.6)
11 FORMAT(1H0)
   RETURN
   END

   SUBROUTINE REPSIM(K,PI1,BIGF,SMLF,U0,UW)
   DIMENSION BIGF(1),SMLF(1),U0(1),UW(1)
   TSTEP=1.0
   ETA1=PI1
   UW(1) = BIGF(1) - ETA1*SMLF(1)*TSTEP*0.5
   UW(2) = BIGF(2) - ETA1*(SMLF(2)+4.0*U0(1)*SMLF(1))*TSTEP/3.0
   UW(3) = BIGF(3) - ETA1*3.0*(SMLF(3)+3.0*U0(1)*SMLF(2)+3.0*U0(2)*
  1        SMLF(1))*TSTEP/8.0
   DO 25 IT=4,K
   IT1 = IT-1
   IF((IT/2)*2.EQ.IT)UW(IT) = SMLF(IT)
   IF((IT/2)*2.NE.IT) UW(IT) = 9.0*(3.0*U0(IT1)*SMLF(1) + 3.0*U0(
  1        IT1-1)*SMLF(2) + U0(IT1-2)*SMLF(3))/8.0 + SMLF(IT)
  2      - U0(IT1-2)*SMLF(3)
   DO 24 J=1,IT1
   IF((IT/2)*2.EQ.IT.AND.(J/2)*2.NE.J) UW(IT) = UW(IT) + 4.0*U0(J)
  1      *SMLF(IT-J)
   IF((IT/2)*2.EQ.IT.AND.(J/2)*2.EQ.J) UW(IT) = UW(IT)+2.0*U0(J)*
  1           SMLF(IT-J)
   IF((IT/2)*2.NE.IT.AND.J.GT.IT-3) GO TO 24
   IF((IT/2)*2.NE.IT.AND.(J/2)*2.NE.J) UW(IT) = UW(IT)+4.0*U0(J)*
  1           SMLF(IT-J)
   IF((IT/2)*2.NE.IT.AND.(J/2)*2.EQ.J) UW(IT) = UW(IT)+2.0*U0(J)*
  1           SMLF(IT-J)
24 CONTINUE
   UW(IT) = BIGF(IT) - ETA1*UW(IT)*TSTEP/3.0
25 CONTINUE
   RETURN
   END


   SUBROUTINE RANL(PI1,C,U,T,HB,XLAM,IPTYPE,IBTYPE,RSMF,
  1USMF,P0)
   DOUBLE PRECISION U,C,T,RSMF,USMF,P,Q,AA,BB,P0,G,BIGH,CU,DU,RR,SS
   IF(IBTYPE-1) 1,1,2
 1 P=(C+1.0)/((C+1.0)**2 + U**2)
   Q=-U/((C+1.0)**2 + U**2)
   GO TO 3
 2 AA=((1.0+2.0*C/XLAM)**2+ 4.0*(U/XLAM)**2)**0.25
   BB=DATAN2(U,C+XLAM/2.0)/2.0
   P=DEXP(XLAM-XLAM*AA*DCOS(BB))*DCOS(XLAM*AA*DSIN(BB))
   Q=-DEXP(XLAM-XLAM*AA*DCOS(BB))*DSIN(XLAM*AA*DSIN(BB))
 3 IF(IPTYPE-2) 4,5,6
 4 P0=DEXP(-DMIN1(50.0D0,T))
   USMF=DEXP(-DMIN1(50.0D0,T-T*P))*DSIN(T*Q)
   RSMF=DEXP(-DMIN1(50.0D0,T-T*P))*DCOS(T*Q)
   GO TO 10
 5 G=((1.0+T/HB-T*P/HB)**2 + (T*Q/HB)**2)**(-HB/2.0)
   BIGH=DATAN2(T*Q,HB+T-T*P)*HB
   CU=G*DCOS(BIGH)
   DU=G*DSIN(BIGH)
   P0=(HB/(T+HB))**HB
   RSMF=CU
   USMF=DU
   GO TO 10
 6 CONTINUE
10 RETURN
   END
```

POLLAK

This calculates $W_n(w)$ by means of (4.8) for Poisson/exponential using two subroutines QG9 and QSF from IBM's SSP. Although the upper limit of n was chosen as 4 in the exhibit this can easily be extended by appropriate change in the DIMENSION statement and in DO loops 10 and 6. Note that w proceeds by tenths of a unit to maintain accuracy but that its upper limit of 100 could be increased. The foregoing increases in n and w have proportional increases in the computing time which was 15 seconds in the program exhibited.

The two EXTERNAL functions correspond to (4.13) and (4.14) and might be substantially more involved for other choices of $p_n(t)$ and $B(\cdot)$.

```
      PROGRAM POLLAK(INPUT,OUTPUT,TAPE5=INPUT,TAPE6=OUTPUT)
      DIMENSION W(4,230),YY(101),ZZ(101),WW(3)
      EXTERNAL FCT,FCTNEG
      WRITE(6,11)
      DO 3 IW=1,100
      W(1,IW)=0.0
      V=FLOAT(IW)/10.
      CALL QG9(0.0,V,FCT,Y)
      CALL QG9(-13.0,0.0,FCTNEG,Z)
      W(1,IW)=Y+Z
    3 CONTINUE
      DO 10 J=1,4
      DO 8 I=101,230
      W(J,I)=1.0
    8 CONTINUE
   10 CONTINUE
C     WW(I) IS W(I,0)
      WW(1)=1.1/2.1
      WRITE(6,13)
      WRITE(6,7) (W(1,I),I=1,100)
.  C  FIRST THE INTEGRAL OVER THE NEGATIVE AXIS. Y0 IS FCT(0.)
      Y0=1.0/2.1
      DO 6 I=2,4
      DO 4 IW=1,100
      W(I,IW)=  W(I-1,IW)*Y0
      DO 5 IX=2,130,2
      X=-FLOAT(IX)/10.
      IW2=IW+IX
      W(I,IW)=W(I,IW)+W(I-1,IW2-1)*FCTNEG(X+.1)*4.+W(I-1,IW2)*FCTNEG(X)*
     1 2.
    5 CONTINUE
      W(I,IW)=(W(I,IW)-  W(I-1,IW+130)*FCTNEG(-13.0))/30.
    4 CONTINUE
      WW(I)=W(I-1)*Y0
      DO 9 IX=2,130,2
      X=-FLOAT(IX)/10.
      WW(I)=WW(I)+ W(  I-1,IX-1)*FCTNEG(X+.1)*4.+W(I-1,IX)*FCTNEG(X)*2.
    9 CONTINUE
      WW(I)=(WW(I)-W(I-1,130)*FCTNEG(-13.0))/30.
      W(I,1)=W(I,1)+.05*(W(I-1,1)*Y0+WW(I-1)*FCT(.1))
C     NOW FOR THE POSITIVE X-VALUES THROUGH IW
      DO 1 IW=2,100
      IW1=IW+1
      DO 2 IX=1,IW1
      X=FLOAT(IX-1)/10.
      IW2=IW-IX+1
      IF(IW2.EQ.0)YY(IX)=WW(I-1)*FCT(X)
      IF(IW2.NE.0) YY(IX)=W(I-1,IW2)*FCT(X)
```

```
  2 CONTINUE
    CALL  QSF(0.1,YY,ZZ,IW1)
    W(I,IW)=W(I,IW)+ZZ(IW1)
  1 CONTINUE
  6 CONTINUE
    WRITE(6,12)
    WRITE(6,14)
    WRITE(6,7)  (W(2,I),I=1,100)
    WRITE(6,12)
    WRITE(6,15)
    WRITE(6,7)  (W(3,I),I=1,100)
    WRITE(6,12)
    WRITE(6,16)
    WRITE(6,7)  (W(4,I),I=1,100)
  7 FORMAT(10E13.6)
 11 FORMAT(1H1)
 12 FORMAT(1H0)
 13 FORMAT(2X,47H100 SURVIVAL PROBABILITIES TO FIRST CLAIM EPOCH)
 14 FORMAT(2X,48H100 SURVIVAL PROBABILITIES TO SECOND CLAIM EPOCH)
 15 FORMAT(2X,47H100 SURVIVAL PROBABILITIES TO THIRD CLAIM EPOCH)
 16 FORMAT(2X,48H100 SURVIVAL PROBABILITIES TO FOURTH CLAIM EPOCH)
    STOP
    END


    FUNCTION FCT(X)
    FCT=EXP(-X)/2.1
    RETURN
    END


    FUNCTION FCTNEG(X)
    FCTNEG=EXP(-ABS(X)/1.1)/2.1
    RETURN
    END


    SUBROUTINE QG9(XL,XU,FCT,Y)
C   REPRINTED BY PERMISSION FROM SYSTEM/360 SCIENTIFIC SUBROUTINE
C   PACKAGE VERSION III(1968) BY INTERNATIONAL BUSINESS MACHINES CORP.
    A=.5*(XU+XL)
    B=XU-XL
    C=.4840801*B
    Y=.04063719*(FCT(A+C)+FCT(A-C))
    C=.4180156*B
    Y=Y+.09032408*(FCT(A+C)+FCT(A-C))
    C=.3066857*B
    Y=Y+.1303053*(FCT(A+C)+FCT(A-C))
    C=.1621267*B
    Y=Y+.1561735*(FCT(A+C)+FCT(A-C))
    Y=B*(Y+.1651197*FCT(A))
    RETURN
    END


    SUBROUTINE QSF(H,Y,Z,NDIM)
C   REPRINTED BY PERMISSION FROM SYSTEM/360 SCIENTIFIC SUBROUTINE
C   PACKAGE VERSION III(1968) BY INTERNATIONAL BUSINESS MACHINES CORP.
    DIMENSION Y(1),Z(1)
    HT=.3333333*H
    IF(NDIM-5) 7,8,1
  1 SUM1=Y(2)+Y(2)
    SUM1=SUM1+SUM1
    SUM1=HT*(Y(1)+SUM1+Y(3))
    AUX1=Y(4)+Y(4)
    AUX1=AUX1+AUX1
    AUX1=SUM1+HT*(Y(3)+AUX1+Y(5))
```

```
      AUX2  =HT*(Y(1)+3.875*(Y(2)+Y(5))+2.625*(Y(3)+Y(4))+Y(6))
      SUM2=Y(5)+Y(5)
      SUM2=SUM2+SUM2
      SUM2=AUX2-HT*(Y(4)+SUM2+Y(6))
      Z(1)=0.
      AUX=Y(3)+Y(3)
      AUX=AUX+AUX
      Z(2)=SUM2-HT*(Y(2)+AUX+Y(4))
      Z(3)=SUM1
      Z(4)=SUM2
      IF(NDIM-6) 5,5,2
    2 DO 4 I=7,NDIM,2
      SUM1=AUX1
      SUM2=AUX2
      AUX1=Y(I-1)+Y(I-1)
      AUX1=AUX1+AUX1
      AUX1=SUM1+HT*(Y(I-2)+AUX1+Y(I))
      Z(I-2)=SUM1
      IF(I-NDIM) 3,5,5
    3 AUX2=Y(I)+Y(I)
      AUX2=AUX2+AUX2
      AUX2=SUM2+HT*(Y(I-1)+AUX2+Y(I+1))
    4 Z(I-1)=SUM2
    5 Z(NDIM-1)=AUX1
      Z(NDIM)=AUX2
      RETURN
    6 Z(NDIM-1)=SUM2
      Z(NDIM)=AUX1
      RETURN
    7 IF(NDIM-3) 12,11,8
    8 SUM2=1.125*HT*(Y(1)+Y(2)+Y(2)+Y(2)+Y(3)+Y(3)+Y(3)+Y(4))
      SUM1=Y(2)+Y(2)
      SUM1=SUM1+SUM1
      SUM1=HT*(Y(1)+SUM1+Y(3))
      Z(1)=0.
      AUX1=Y(3)+Y(3)
      AUX1=AUX1+AUX1
      Z(2)=SUM2-HT*(Y(2)+AUX1+Y(4))
      IF(NDIM-5) 10,9,9
    9 AUX1=Y(4)+Y(4)
      AUX1=AUX1+AUX1
      Z(5)=SUM1+HT*(Y(3)+AUX1+Y(5))
   10 Z(3)=SUM1
      Z(4)=SUM2
      RETURN
   11 SUM1=HT*(1.25*Y(1)+Y(2)+Y(2)-.25*Y(3))
      SUM2=Y(2)+Y(2)
      SUM2=SUM2+SUM2
      Z(3)=HT*(Y(1)+SUM2+Y(3))
      Z(1)=0.
      Z(2)=SUM1
   12 RETURN
      END
```

DEMUWT

This is an extension of DEMOIV to provide check values of $U(w, t)$. The number of integer t-values is given by ITTOP, the premium rate ($1 + \eta$ when the net is unity) is punched PI1, and w must be selected. The b_j's are calculated by the user and $p_n(t)$ must be programmed for every t and for the relevant values of n for given t. The 100 loop concludes the user's choices.

```
      PROGRAM DEMUWT(INPUT,OUTPUT,TAPE5 =INPUT,TAPE6=OUTPUT)
      DIMENSION B(79),X(80),Y(300),Z(300)
      DIMENSION P(50,25),ICONV(25),P0(25)
      DIMENSION F(300,25),SF(300,25)
      DIMENSION U0(25),UW(25)
      DIMENSION BIGF(25),SMLF(25)
      WRITE(6,1)
      E=(2.7182818285)**0.2

C     ITTOP IS THE NUMBER OF INTEGER T-VALUES

      ITTOP=25
      PI1=1.0
      W=50.0

C     CALCULATE SMALL B(.) AND ITS SUM

      EMILAM=0.8
      B(1)=1.0-EMILAM
      DO 3 J=2,79
      B(J)=EMILAM*B(J-1)
    3 CONTINUE
      SUM=0.0
      DO 11 J=1,79
      SUM=SUM+B(J)
   11 CONTINUE
      WRITE(6,194)
      WRITE(6,5) B
      WRITE(6,204) SUM
      B0=0.0

      IDIMX=80
      X(1)=B0
      DO 198 J=2,IDIMX
      X(J)=B(J-1)
      Y(J)=X(J)
  198 CONTINUE
      IDIMY=IDIMX
      ISTART=0
      WRITE(6,2)

C     CALCULATE P(N,T) AND ITS UPPER ABSCISSA ICONV(IT)

      DO 100 IT=1,ITTOP
      T=FLOAT(IT)/5.0
      P0(IT)=EXP(-AMIN1(T,30.0))
      PT=1.0
      DO 10 J=1,IT
      PT=PT*T/(E*FLOAT(J))
   10 CONTINUE
      P(IT,IT)=PT
      IT1=IT-1
      DO 6 J=1,IT1
      J1=IT-J
      P(J1,IT)=P(J1+1,IT)*FLOAT(IT+1-J)/T
    6 CONTINUE
      DO 8 J=1,100
      K=J+IT1
      L=J+IT
      P(L,IT)=P(K,IT)*T/FLOAT(IT+J)

      IF(P(L,IT).LT.4.0E-8) GO TO 12
    8 CONTINUE
   12 CONTINUE
      ICONV(IT) = J+IT-1
      NTOP=ICONV(ITTOP)
  100 CONTINUE
```

```
C       THE PRINT-OUT FOR ANY N IS THE NTH CONVOLUTION,N=2,3,... OF B(.)

        DO 199 N=1,NTOP
        IF(N.EQ.1) GO TO   206
        DO 200 JJ=1,IDIMZ
        IF(Z(JJ) .GT.4.0E-8) IFIRST=JJ
        IF(Z(JJ) .GT.4.0E-8)  GO TO 201
    200 CONTINUE
    201 DO 202 JK=1,IDIMZ
        JJJ=IDIMZ-JK+1
        IF(Z(JJJ).GT.4.0E-8) ILAST=JJJ
        IF(Z(JJJ).GT.4.0E-8) GO TO 203
    202 CONTINUE
    203 IDIMY=ILAST-IFIRST+1
        IFIR1=IFIRST-1
        ISTART=ISTART+IFIR1
        WRITE(6,197) N
        WRITE(6,196) ISTART
        WRITE(6,207) (Z(L),L=IFIRST,ILAST)
        WRITE(6,2)

C       CALCULATE CONTRIBUTION TO SMLF(X,T)

        IBOT=ISTART
        ITOP=ISTART+ILAST-IFIRST
        DO 101 IC=1,ITTOP
        IF(N.GT.ICONV(IC)) GO TO 101
        DO 211 IX=IBOT,ITOP

C       THE I-VALUES RUN FROM IFIRST TO ILAST

        I=IX-IBOT+IFIRST
        F(IX,IC)=F(IX,IC) + P(N,IC)*Z(I)
    211 CONTINUE
    101 CONTINUE
        IF(N .EQ.NTOP) GO TO 199
        DO 205 JL=1,IDIMY
        JM=IFIRST+JL-1
        Y(JL)=Z(JM)
    205 CONTINUE
    206 CALL PMPY(Z,IDIMZ,X,IDIMX,Y,IDIMY)
    199 CONTINUE
        DO 102 IC=1,ITTOP
        DO 210 IX=1,79
        F(IX,IC)=F(IX,IC) + P(1,IC)*B(IX)
    210 CONTINUE

C       CALCULATE BIGF(X,T)

        SF(1,IC)=F(1,IC) + P0(IC)
        DO 212 IX=2,ITOP
        SF(IX,IC)=SF(IX-1,IC) + F(IX,IC)
    212 CONTINUE
        WRITE(6,195) IC
        WRITE(6,207) (F(L,IC),L=1,ITOP)
        WRITE(6,2)
        WRITE(6,207) P0(IC)
        WRITE(6,207) (SF(L,IC),L=1,ITOP)
        WRITE(6,2)
        WRITE(6,2)
    102 CONTINUE

C       CALCULATE U(0,T)

        DO 300 JT=1,ITTOP
        T=FLOAT(JT)
```

```
      SUMSF=P0(JT)
      DO 301 JJ=1,JT
      SUMSF=SUMSF+SF(JJ,JT)
  301 CONTINUE
      SUMSF=SUMSF - 0.5*(P0(JT) + SF(JT,JT))
      U0(JT) = SUMSF/T
  300 CONTINUE

C     CALCULATE U(W,T)

      DO 302 J=1,ITTOP
      BIGF(J)=SF(J+W,J)
      SMLF(J)=F(J+W,J)
  302 CONTINUE
      CALL REPSIM(ITTOP,PI1,BIGF,SMLF,U0,UW)
      WRITE(6,215)
      WRITE(6,5) (U0(L),L=5,25,5)
      WRITE(6,2)
      WRITE(6,216)
      WRITE(6,5) (UW(L),L=5,25,5)
    1 FORMAT(1H1)
    2 FORMAT(1H0)
    5 FORMAT(1H ,10E13.5)
  194 FORMAT(2X,18HTHE DENSITIES B(.))
  195 FORMAT(2X,36HTHE ARRAYS SMLF AND BIGF FOR T EQUAL   I4)
  196 FORMAT(2X,25HSTARTING NUMBER OF CLAIMS   I4)
  197 FORMAT(2X,15HCONVOLUTION NO.   I4)
  204 FORMAT(2X,E15.8)
  207 FORMAT(2X,10E13.6)
  208 FORMAT(2X,I6)
  215 FORMAT(2X,13HU(0,T) VALUES)
  216 FORMAT(2X,13HU(W,T) VALUES)
      STOP
      END


      SUBROUTINE PMPY(Z,IDIMZ,X,IDIMX,Y,IDIMY)
C     REPRINTED BY PERMISSION FROM SYSTEM/360 SCIENTIFIC SUBROUTINE
C     PACKAGE VERSION III(1968) BY INTERNATIONAL BUSINESS MACHINES CORP.
      DIMENSION Z(1),X(IDIMX),Y(IDIMY)
      IF(IDIMX*IDIMY) 10,10,20
   10 IDIMZ=0
      GO TO 50
   20 IDIMZ=IDIMX+IDIMY-1
      DO 30 I=1,IDIMZ
   30 Z(I)=0.0
      DO 40 I=1,IDIMX
      DO 40 J=1,IDIMY
      K=I+J-1
   40 Z(K)=X(I)*Y(J)+Z(K)
   50 RETURN
      END


      SUBROUTINE REPSIM(K,PI1,BIGF,SMLF,U0,UW)
      DIMENSION BIGF(1),SMLF(1),U0(1),UW(1)
      TSTEP=1.0
      ETA1=PI1
      UW(1) = BIGF(1) - ETA1*SMLF(1)*TSTEP*0.5
      UW(2) = BIGF(2) - ETA1*(SMLF(2)+4.0*U0(1)*SMLF(1))*TSTEP/3.0
      UW(3) = BIGF(3) - ETA1*3.0*(SMLF(3)+3.0*U0(1)*SMLF(2)+3.0*U0(2)*
     1          SMLF(1))*TSTEP/8.0
      DO 25 IT=4,K
      IT1 = IT-1
      IF((IT/2)*2.EQ.IT)UW(IT) = SMLF(IT)
      IF((IT/2)*2.NE.IT) UW(IT) = 9.0*(3.0*U0(IT1)*SMLF(1) + 3.0*U0(
     1          IT1-1)*SMLF(2) + U0(IT1-2)*SMLF(3))/8.0 + SMLF(IT)
```

```
  2     - U0(IT1-2)*SMLF(3)
     DO 24 J=1,IT1
     IF((IT/2)*2.EQ.IT.AND.(J/2)*2.NE.J) UW(IT) = UW(IT) + 4.0*U0(J)
    1      *SMLF(IT-J)
     IF((IT/2)*2.EQ.IT.AND.(J/2)*2.EQ.J) UW(IT) = UW(IT)+2.0*U0(J)*
    1          SMLF(IT-J)
     IF((IT/2)*2.NE.IT.AND.J.GT.IT-3) GO TO 24
     IF((IT/2)*2.NE.IT.AND.(J/2)*2.NE.J) UW(IT) = UW(IT)+4.0*U0(J)*
    1          SMLF(IT-J)
     IF((IT/2)*2.NE.IT.AND.(J/2)*2.EQ.J) UW(IT) = UW(IT)+2.0*U0(J)*
    1          SMLF(IT-J)
 24  CONTINUE
     UW(IT) = BIGF(IT) - ETA1*UW(IT)*TSTEP/3.0
 25  CONTINUE
     RETURN
     END
```

UINTEG

This program calculates the probability of eternal survival, $U(w)$, by means of Cramér's integral equation (5.3) which assumes that $p_n(t)$ is Poisson. The accuracy depends strongly on the value assumed for H and this is discussed in Chapter 5.

```
     PROGRAM UINTEG(INPUT,OUTPUT,TAPE5=INPUT,TAPE6=OUTPUT)
     DIMENSION UINF( 400),HH( 400),BEBO( 400)
     ALPH2=0.3306*SQRT(2.0)
     BET2=-1.9569*SQRT(2.0)
     P1=        EXP((1.-2.*ALPH2*BET2)/(2.*ALPH2*ALPH2))
     P2=EXP((2.0-2.0*ALPH2*BET2)/ALPH2**2)
     P3=EXP((9.0-6.0*ALPH2*BET2)/(ALPH2**2*2.0))
     P2=P2/(P1*P1)
     P3=P3/(P1*P1*P1)
     P1=1.0
     WRITE(6,401) P2,P3
     SIGMA=SQRT(ALOG(P2/(P1*P1)))
     ZETA=ALOG(P1*P1/SQRT(P2))
     WRITE(6,401) SIGMA,ZETA
     WRITE(6,101)
     H=0.001
     TSTEP = H
     NN=400
     DO 1 J=1,NN
     Z=(ALOG(FLOAT(J)*H)- ZETA)/SIGMA
     CALL BIGPHI(Z,F)
     HH(J)=(1.-F)/1.1
  1  CONTINUE
 C   SEAL(1969) 4.43. HH IS H AND UINF IS PHI
     PI1=1.1
     A=0.1/PI1
     U0=0.1/PI1
     HH0=1.0/PI1
     CALL INTEON(A,PI1,H,NN,HH,U0,HH0,UINF)
     WRITE(6,401) UINF
     WRITE(6,402)
     BET=2.*P3/(3.*P2) + P2*(1.-.1/P1)/0.2
     ALPH=P2*(0.1+P1)/(2.0*0.1*BET*P1)
     DO 4 I=1,400
     W=FLOAT(I)*H*P1/BET
     CALL GAB(ALPH,W,G)
     CALL GMMMA(ALPH,GX, IER)
```

```
      GB=G/GX
      BEBO(I)=.1/1.1 +GB/1.1
    4 CONTINUE
      WRITE(6,401) BEBO
  101 FORMAT(1H1)
  401 FORMAT(1H ,10E13.6)
  402 FORMAT(1H0)
      STOP
      END


      SUBROUTINE INTEQN(A,PI1,H,NN,HH,U0,HH0,UINF)
      DIMENSION UINF(1),HH(1)
      TSTEP=H
      UINF(1)=(A+H*U0*HH(1)/2.0)/(1.0-H*HH0/2.0)
      UINF(2)=(    A    +H*(4.0*UINF(1)*HH(1) +      U0  *HH(2))/3.)/(1.-
     1H*HH0/3.0)
      UINF(3)=(    A    + 3.*H*(3.*UINF(2)*HH(1)+3.*UINF(1)*HH(2)+
     1 U0 *HH(3))/8.)/(1.-3.*H*HH0/8.0)
      DO 25 IT=4,NN
      IT1 = IT-1
      IF((IT/2)*2.EQ.IT)UINF(IT)=A*3.0/H + U0*HH(IT)
      IF((IT/2)*2.NE.IT)UINF(IT)= 9.0*(3.0*HH(IT1)*UINF(1)  + 3.0*HH(
     1         IT1-1)*UINF(2) + HH(IT1-2)*UINF(3))/8.0
     2      - HH(IT1-2)*UINF(3) +     A    *(3.0/TSTEP)+9.*HH(IT)*U0/8.
      DO 24 J=1,IT1
      IF((IT/2)*2.EQ.IT.AND.(J/2)*2.NE.J)UINF(IT)=UINF(IT)+ 4.0*HH(J)*
     1         *UINF(IT-J)
      IF((IT/2)*2.EQ.IT.AND.(J/2)*2.EQ.J)UINF(IT)=UINF(IT)+2.*HH(J)*
     1             UINF(IT-J)
      IF((IT/2)*2.NE.IT.AND.J.GT.IT-3) GO TO 24
      IF((IT/2)*2.NE.IT.AND.(J/2)*2.NE.J)UINF(IT)=UINF(IT)+4.*HH(J)*
     1           UINF(IT-J)
      IF((IT/2)*2.NE.IT.AND.(J/2)*2.EQ.J)UINF(IT)=UINF(IT)+2.*HH(J)*
     1           UINF(IT-J)
   24 CONTINUE
      UINF(IT)=UINF(IT)*TSTEP/(3.*(1.-H*HH0/3.0))
   25 CONTINUE
      RETURN
      END


      SUBROUTINE BIGPHI(Y,F)
      AY=ABS(Y)
      T = 1.0/(1.0+.2316419*AY)
      F = 1.330274429
      F = F*T - 1.821255978
      F = F*T + 1.781477937
      F = F*T - .356563782
      F = F*T + .319381530
      F = F*T
      D=0.398942280*EXP(-Y*Y/2.0)
      F=F*D
      IF(Y) 1,2,2
    2 F=1.0-F
    1 RETURN
      END


      SUBROUTINE GMMMA(XX,GX,IER)
C     REPRINTED BY PERMISSION FROM SYSTEM/360 SCIENTIFIC SUBROUTINE
C     PACKAGE VERSION III(1968) BY INTERNATIONAL BUSINESS MACHINES CORP.
      IF(XX-57.) 6,6,4
    4 IER=2
      GX=1.E75
      RETURN
    6 X=XX
      ERR=1.0E-6
```

```
      IER=0
      GX=1.0
      IF(X-2.0) 50,50,15
   10 IF(X-2.0) 110,110,15
   15 X=X-1.0
      GX=GX*X
      GO TO 10
   50 IF(X-1.0) 60,120,110
   60 IF(X-ERR) 62,62,80
   62 Y=FLOAT(INT(X))-X
      IF(ABS(Y)-ERR) 130,130,64
   64 IF(1.0-Y-ERR) 130,130,70
   70 IF(X-1.0) 80,80,110
   80 GX=GX/X
      X=X+1.0
      GO TO 70
  110 Y=X-1.0
      GY=1.0+Y*(-0.5771017+Y*(+.9858540+Y*(-0.8764218+Y*(+0.8328212+
     1Y*(-0.5684729+Y*(+0.2548205+Y*(-0.05149930))))))))
      GX=GX*GY
  120 RETURN
  130 IER=1
      RETURN
      END




      SUBROUTINE GAB(A,B,G)
C     FORMULA (11) OF KHAMIS(1965) MULTIPLIED BY GAMMA(A)
C     PRODUCES P(A,B) TO 7 DECIMALS WITH OCCASIONAL LAST PL. UNIT ERROR
      TERM = 1.0/A
      P=B**A*EXP(A)
      Q=A**A*EXP(B)
      SUM = TERM
      DO 1 K=1,50
      TERM = TERM*B/(A+FLOAT(K))
      IF(P*TERM/Q.LE.4.0E-08) GO TO 2
      SUM = SUM + TERM
    1 CONTINUE
    2 G = SUM*B**A*EXP(-B)
      RETURN
      END
```

Bibliography

Ammeter, H. (1948). A generalization of the collective theory of risk in regard to fluctuating basic-probabilities. *Skand. Aktu. Tidskr.*, **31**, 171–198.

Amoroso, E. (1942). Nuove ricerche intorno alla distribuzione delle malattie per durata. *Atti Ist. Naz. Assic.*, **14**, 185–202.

Amoroso, L. (1934). La rappresentazione analitica delle curve di frequenza nei sinistri di infortuni e di responsabilitá civile. *Atti X Cong. Inter. Attu.*, **3**, 458–472.

Arfwedson, G. (1950). Some problems in the collective theory of risk. *Skand. Aktu. Tidskr.*, **33**, 1–38.

Atkinson, K. E. (1976). *A Survey of Numerical Methods for the Solution of Fredholm Integral Equations of the Second Kind.* S.I.A.M., Philadelphia, Pa.

Bagchi, T.P. and Templeton, J. G. C. (1972). *Numerical Methods in Markov Chains and Bulk Queues.* Springer–Verlag, Berlin.

Bailey, A. L. (1943). Sampling theory in casualty insurance. Parts III through VII. *Proc. Casualty Actu. Soc.*, **30**, 31–65.

Barrois, T. (1835). Essai sur l'application du calcul des probabilités aux assurances contre l'incendie. *Mem. Soc. Roy. Sci. Agric. Arts de Lille*, 1834, 85–282.

Beard, R. E. (1971). On the calculation of the ruin probability for a finite time period. *Astin Bull.*, **6**, 129–133.

Beard, R. E. (1975). Ruin probability during a finite time interval. *Astin Bull.*, **8**, 265–271.

Beekman, J. A. (1969). A ruin function approximation. *Trans. Soc. Actu.*, **21**, 41–48, 275–279.

Beekman, J. A., and Bowers, N. L., Jr. (1972). An approximation to the finite time ruin function. *Skand. Aktu. Tidskr.*, **55**, 41–56, 128–137.

Benckert, L.-G. (1962). The lognormal model for the distribution of one claim. *Astin Bull.*, **2**, 9–23.

Beneš, V. E. (1963). *General Stochastic Processes in the Theory of Queues.* Addison–Wesley, Reading, Mass.

Benktander, G. (1970). Schadenverteilung nach Grösse in der Nicht-Leben-Versicherung. *Mitt. Verein. Schweiz. Versich. Mathr.*, **70**, 263–284.

Bhat, U. N. (1972). *Elements of Applied Stochastic Processes.* Wiley, New York.

Bohlmann, G., and Motel, H. Poterin du (1909). Technique de l'assurance sur la vie. *Encyc. Sci. Math.*, *I*, **4**, 491–590.

Bohman, H., and Esscher, F. (1963–64). Studies in risk theory with numerical illustrations concerning distribution functions and stop loss premiums. *Skand. Aktu. Tidskr.*, **46**, 173–225; **47**, 1–40.

Bühlmann, H., and Hartmann, W. (1956). Änderungen in der Grundgesamtheit der Betriebsunfallkosten. *Mitt. Verein. Schweiz. Versich. Mathr.*, 56, 303–320.

Cannella, S. (1963). Variation de la prime d'assurance de l'assistance pharmaceutique en fonction de la participation de l'assuré au coût de l'assistance. *Astin Bull.*, 2, 30–44.

Clendenin, W. W. (1966). A method for numerical calculation of Fourier integrals. *Numer. Math.*, 8, 422–436.

Cohen, J. W. (1969). *The Single Server Queue*. North-Holland, Amsterdam.

Cramér, H. (1930). On the mathematical theory of risk. pp. 7–84 of *Festskrift Försäkringsaktiebolaget Skandia*. Stockholm.

Cramér, H. (1945). *Mathematical Methods of Statistics*. Almqvist and Wiksell, Stockholm.

Cramér, H. (1955). Collective Risk Theory. Jubilee Volume of *Försäkringsaktiebolaget Skandia*, Stockholm.

Cramér, H. (1969). Historical review of Filip Lundberg's works on risk theory. *Skand. Aktu. Tidskr.*, 52, *Suppl.*, 6–12.

Davis, P. J., and Rabinowitz, P. (1975). *Methods of Numerical Integration*. Academic Press, New York.

De Moivre, A. (1718, 1738, 1756). *The Doctrine of Chances*. Millar, London.

Dormoy, E. (1878). *Théorie Mathématique des Assurances sur la Vie*. Paris.

Dropkin, L. B. (1966). *Loss distributions of a single claim*. Author's Mimeograph.

Dubner, H., and Abate, J. (1968). Numerical inversion of Laplace transforms by relating them to the finite Fourier cosine transform. *J. Assoc. Comput. Mach.*, 15, 115–123.

Einarsson, B. (1972). Algorithm 418. Calculation of Fourier integrals. *Comm. Assoc. Comput. Mach.*, 15, 47–48.

Erlang, A. K. (1909). Sandsynlighedsregning og telefonsamtaler. *Nyt Tidskr. Mat. B*, 20, 33–40. [English trans. in Brockmeyer, E. *et al.*, *The Life and Works of A. K. Erlang*, Copenhagen Telephone Co., Copenhagen.]

Ferrara, G. (1971). Distributions des sinistres incendie selon leur coût. *Astin Bull.*, 6, 31–41.

Gani, J., and Prabhu, N. U. (1959). Remarks on the dam with Poisson type inputs. *Aust. J. Appl. Sci.*, 10, 113–122.

Grandell, J., and Segerdahl, C.-O. (1971). A comparison of some approximations of ruin probabilities. *Skand. Aktu. Tidskr.*, 54, 143–158.

Gross, D., and Harris, C. M. (1974). *Fundamentals of Queueing Theory*. Wiley, New York.

Irwin, J. O. (1968). The generalized Waring distribution applied to accident theory. *J. Roy. Statist. Soc. A.*, 130, 205–225.

Irwin, J. O. (1975). The generalized Waring distribution. *J. Roy. Statist. Soc. A*, 138, 18–31, 204–227, 374–384.

Johnson, N. L., and Kotz, S. (1970). *Continuous Univariate Distributions – 1*. Houghton Mifflin, Boston.

Kauppi, L., and Ojantakanen, P. (1969). Approximations of the generalized Poisson function. *Astin Bull.*, 5, 213–226.

Kendall, D. G. (1951). Some problems in the theory of queues. *J. Roy. Statist. Soc. B*, 13, 151–185.

Kendall, D. G. (1953). Stochastic processes occurring in the theory of queues and their analysis by the method of the imbedded Markov chain. *Ann. Math. Statist.*, 24, 338–354.

Kendall, M. G., and Stuart, A. (1977). *The Advanced Theory of Statistics*, Vol. 1., Griffin, London.

Khamis, S. H., with Rudert, W. (1965). *Tables of the Incomplete Gamma Function Ratio.* von Liebig, Darmstadt.

Khintchine, A. (1933). *Asymptotische Gesetze der Wahrscheinlichkeitsrechnung.* Springer, Berlin.

Krylov, V. I., and Skoblya, N. S. (1969). *Handbook of Numerical Inversion of Laplace Transforms.* Israel Program for Scientific Translation, Jerusalem.

Laurin, I. (1930). An introduction into Lundberg's theory of risk. *Skand. Aktu. Tidskr.,* **13**, 84–111.

Lindley, D. V. (1952). The theory of queues with a single server. *Proc. Camb. Philos. Soc.,* **48**, 277–289.

Luke, Y. L. (1975). *Mathematical Functions and their Approximations.* Academic Press, New York.

Lundberg, F. (1903). I. *Approximerad Framställning af Sannolikhetsfunktionen.* II. *Återförsäkring af Kollektivrisker.* Almqvist and Wiksell, Uppsala.

Lundberg, F. (1909). *Über die Theorie der Rückversicherung, VI. Internat. Kong. f. Versich.-Wissenschaft,* I, 877–955.

Lundberg, F. (1919). *Försäkringsbolags Fondbildning och Riskutjämning.* II. *Teori för Riskmassor.* Beckman, Stockholm.

Lundberg, O. (1940). *On Random Processes and their Application to Sickness and Accident Statistics.* Almqvist and Wiksell, Uppsala.

McFadden, J. A. (1962). On the lengths of intervals in a stationary point process. *J. Roy. Statist. Soc. B,* **24**, 364–382, 500.

Nance, R. E., Bhat, U. N., and Claybrook, B. G. (1972). Busy period analysis of a time-sharing system: Transform inversion. *J. Assoc. Comput. Mach.,* **19**, 453–463.

Neuts, M. F. (1976). *An Annotated Bibliography of Computational Probability* – Part I. Purdue University, Dept. Statist., Div. Math. Sci., Mimeo. No. 443.

Olver, F. W. J. (1964). Bessel functions of integer order. *Handbook of Mathematical Functions.* Nat. Bur. Standards, Washington, D.C.

Prabhu, N. U. (1961). On the ruin problem of collective risk theory. *Ann. Math. Statist.,* **32**, 757–764.

Prabhu, N. U. (1965). *Queues and Inventories.* Wiley, New York.

Reich, E. (1961). Some combinatorial theorems for continuous parameter processes. *Math. Scand.,* **9**, 243–257.

Riordan, J. (1968). *Combinatorial Identities.* Wiley, New York.

Ryder, J. M. (1976). Subjectivism – A reply in defence of classical actuarial methods. *J. Inst. Actu.,* **103**, 59–112.

Saaty, T. L. (1961). *Elements of Queueing Theory.* McGraw-Hill, New York.

Seal, H. L. (1949). The historical development of the use of generating functions in probability theory. *Mitt. Verein. Schweiz. Versich. Mathr.,* **49**, 209–228. Reprinted in: Kendall, M., and Plackett, R. L., *Studies in the History of Statistics and Probability.* Griffin, London, 1977.

Seal, H. L. (1969). *Stochastic Theory of a Risk Business.* Wiley, New York.

Seal, H. L. (1969a). Simulation of the ruin potential of non-life insurance companies. *Trans. Soc. Actu.,* **21**, 563–590.

Seal, H. L. (1971). Numerical calculation of the Bohman-Esscher family of convolution-mixed negative binomial distribution functions. *Mitt. Verein. Schweiz. Versich. Mathr.,* **71**, 71–94.

Seal, H. L. (1972a). Numerical calculation of the probability of ruin in the Poisson/exponential case. *Mitt. Verein. Schweitz. Versich. Mathr.,* **72**, 141–164.

Seal, H. L. (1972b). Risk theory and the single-server queue. *Mitt. Verein. Schweiz. Versich. Mathr.*, **72**, 171–178.

Seal, H. L. (1974). The numerical calculation of $U(w, t)$, the probability of non-ruin in an interval $(0, t)$. *Scand. Actu. J.*, 1974, 121–139.

Seal, H. L. (1975). A note on the use of Laguerre polynomials in the inversion of Laplace transforms. *Bl. Deutsch. Ges. Versich. Math.*, **12**, 131–134.

Seal, H. L. (1977a). Approximations to risk theory's $F(x, t)$ by means of the gamma distribution. *Astin Bull.*, **9**, 213–218.

Seal, H. L. (1977b). Numerical inversion of characteristic functions. *Scand. Actu. J.*, 1977, 48–53.

Seal, H. L. (1978). From aggregate claims distribution to probability of ruin. *Astin Bull.*, **10**, 47–53.

Segerdahl, C.-O. (1970). Stochastic processes and practical working models or Why is the Polya process approach defective in modern practice and how cope with its deficiencies? *Skand. Aktu. Tidskr.*, **53**, 146–166.

Squire, W. (1970). *Integration for Engineers and Scientists*. American Elsevier, New York.

Steffensen, J. F. (1927). *Interpolation*. Williams and Wilkins, Baltimore, Md. (Reprinted 1950 by Dover, New York.)

Stehfest, H. (1970). Numerical inversion of Laplace transforms. *Comm. Assoc. Comput. Mach.*, **13**, 47–49.

Stroud, A. H., and Secrest, D. (1966). *Gaussian Quadrature Formulas*. Prentice-Hall, Englewood Cliffs, N.J.

Takács, L. (1962). *Introduction to the Theory of Queues*. Oxford Univ. Press, New York.

Thyrion, P. (1959). Sur une propriété des processus de Poisson généralisés. *Bull. Ass. Roy. Actu. Belges*, **59**, 35–46.

Thyrion, P. (1969). Extension of the collective risk theory. *Skand. Actu. Tidskr.*, **52**, Suppl., 84–98.

Thyrion, P. (1971/2). Remarques sur la transformation d'une famille de lois de Poisson composées en lois de Poisson par grappes. *Astin Bull.*, **6**, 47–53.

Tuck, E. O. (1967). A simple 'Filon-trapezoidal' rule. *Math. Comp.*, **21**, 239–241.

Vooren, A. I., van de, and Linde, H. J. van (1966). Numerical calculation of integrals with strongly oscillating integrand. *Math. Comp.*, **20**, 232–245.

Index